AIDA Europe Research Series on Insurance Law and Regulation

Volume 17

The AIDA Europe Research Series on Insurance Law and Regulation is the first book series of its kind and area of specialization. It comprises volumes on topics researched and written with an international, comparative or European perspective.

The regulatory response to the financial crisis in 2008 has pushed towards the adoption of transnational principles and rules also in the field of insurance by encouraging the convergence of national regulations to common regulatory framework. The need for a common legal language emerges to fully understand the process of transnational convergence in place and its impact on national legislation. On the other hand, persisting national peculiarities must be examined in the light of the transnational convergence of rules and concepts. Moreover, new risks, business practices and customers' issues are emerging worldwide, so requiring increasingly global responses.

The scope of the series is to bring together academics, practitioners and policy makers in order to exchange views and approaches to the topics concerned, which are based on the new transnational dimension of insurance law, business and regulation. All contributions are peer reviewed.

Dorota Maśniak

The Legal Framework for the Use of Insurance in Ecological Waste Management

Springer

Dorota Maśniak
University of Gdansk
Gdańsk, Poland

ISSN 2662-1770 ISSN 2662-1789 (electronic)
AIDA Europe Research Series on Insurance Law and Regulation
ISBN 978-3-032-26549-4 ISBN 978-3-032-26550-0 (eBook)
https://doi.org/10.1007/978-3-032-26550-0

This Springer imprint is published by the registered company Springer Nature Switzerland AG
The registered company address is: Gewerbestrasse 11, 6330 Cham, Switzerland

Mojej kochanej mamie z wdzięcznością

Contents

Introduction

1 A Philosophical and Linguistic Analysis of *Waste*

In dogmatic research, conceptual precision is an essential prerequisite for any systematic and normative analysis. Beginning this work with a philosophical and linguistic analysis of the term "waste" provides a solid conceptual foundation for further legal reasoning. The term "waste," as used by EU legislators and more broadly in environmental law, is a complex cultural, temporal, and ontological category. Its meaning has evolved over the centuries—from denoting vast emptiness and abandonment (Latin: vastus) to describing excess materials and their disuse. This semantic evolution reflects deeper changes in the human approach to nature, time, and value.

Various terms are used to denote objects that are not used anymore: waste, rubbish, trash, garbage. The choice of the term "waste" to describe insurance risks (referred to in the waste risks monograph) and the type of insurance relating to these risks (referred to in the waste insurance monograph) stems from the use of this term as a legal term by the EU legislator. The term "waste" carries with it complex associations with landscape, the divine, human sovereignty and proportion. The word "waste" comes from "vastus" deriving from the same Latin root as the word "vast" and meaning the time and space that is void, immense or enormous.[1] The earliest use of the word "waste" referred to a vast, empty and significantly depopulated landscape of "uninhabited" (or sparsely inhabited) and uncultivated country, a wild and desolate region, a desert, wilderness.[2] The status of waste is relative, which does not facilitate the identification of the risks associated with its management and the choice of an appropriate instrument to protect against their materialisation. The

[1] Instead of many Viney (2014), p. 10.

[2] The Oxford English Dictionary, 2nd 1989. s.v. 'waste'.

D. Maśniak, *The Legal Framework for the Use of Insurance in Ecological Waste Management*, AIDA Europe Research Series on Insurance Law and Regulation 17, https://doi.org/10.1007/978-3-032-26550-0_1

philosophical perspective also indicates two factors that support considering waste: space and time. M. Douglas uses the term "matter out of place" referring it to the concept of dirt and arguing that "concept of dirt and the dirty are intimately linked to how we think with act in space".[3] Douglas claims that our classification of dirt is not based on what the objects are, but where they are and what is our attitude towards them.

The time strongly influences our experience of and dealings with waste things. As W. Viney writes, waste is also a "matter out of time". Waste is also matter for which time has run out or has become precluded. Discarded objects are sometimes said to have "had their time" and that's might therefore be disposed of. Time conditions waste and provides a measure of our actions. Waste is also matter that lingers and remains; it is that category of things conspicuous for coming to be by having been. Use-time is a time of wearing, emptying, digesting, breaking or exhausting—a time of diminishing potential, a time oriented to and by an end. The etymology of waste contains a sense of a temporal severance, abandonment or exclusion, a time lacking the orientating shape of use-time. This territorial notion of waste exceeds more modern associations than tend to stress human agency and creation. Environmental depletion is space that gain definition from the productive time that it cannot use to the human purposes to which it is not projected.

Etymological evolution of the term "waste" shows that it is not simply something which comes after another event or is easily thrown in the bin, but helps describe an ancient relationship between humans, material and time. It is a conception of waste that has at its first step the separation and temporal organization of things. Common to both prior and posterior forms of waste are two quite distinct ideas -immensity and emptiness. The temporality of waste is a condition of both, an a priori emptiness and a thing that has become empty. It is both a pre-existing desert and a space that was once but is no longer inhabited, a site of origin and end. W. Viney points out that the etymology of the word "vaste" includes a sense of temporary separation, abandonment or exclusion, "time lacking the orientating shape of use-time". The waste establishes estranged relationships within an object, a temporal break of its use and non-use. Simultaneously, these are the relationships that help to recognize something as "waste".

Economists, however, tend to think of waste as a "negative externality", that is something that occurs as an indirect consequence of a process or exchange.[4] This economically limited idea is popular in the social sciences. According to a deterministic understanding of waste, waste is all that can be bought, used and discarded. According to Rogers, waste is considered to be "intrinsic to consumption". The social history of waste is only 200 years old and is linked to consumer culture.[5] Impact of industrialization was to produce waste as a contemporary thing.[6]

---

[3] Douglas (2002), p. 44.

[4] Laffont (2008).

[5] Strasser (1999), p. 17, 18.

[6] Rogers (2006), p. 31, 50.

With a slightly different emphasis on the idea of the commodity, Julian Stallabrass highlights how, by manipulating desire, the commodity fetish motivates and intensifies our production of waste. For Stallabrass, when objects cease to function they shed their arbitrary act as commodities. By becoming waste these objects are released from commodity fetish, driven by the predominance of exchange-value, in order to reveal how things "really are/were".[7]

Greg Kennedy presents a theory of waste through phenomenological tradition. Kennedy argues that our capacity to discard things is a unique reminder of our own finitude: "understanding thrash brings us closer to ourselves". It discloses our humanity.[8] Predicted on the belief that care is intrinsic to human behaviour, Kennedy argues that "wasting is somehow anti-human, betraying a more intrinsic and original relation with material things".[9] As Harman explains, "the more efficiently the tool performs its function, the more it tends to recede from view".[10] When its unusability is thus discovered, equipment becomes conspicuous. The advent of waste puts objects at a threshold by which pre-existing structures of meaning are called forth to expose their fragility.[11] In Heidegger's philosophy of things, the temporality of the broken tool and the event it produces keep waste from negating meaning. The object does not simply disappear but it becomes ready-to hand in a new way.[12]

According to Bill Brown (author of the Thing Theory[13]) interruption to utility might provoke a reconsideration of an object. In his view, "we began to confront the thingness of objects when they stop working for us". Brown suggests that we come to know an object in a new way when we can no longer put it to use. This permits a confrontation with what he calls "the thingness" of the object disclosing our compulsion to master and manipulate things, asserting a material presence that is somehow outside our control. When things break they expose us to a world of matter. Waste exposes a certain state of affairs by casting a "subject-object relation" into the past, into the realm of the no longer. Brown emphasises that "the thing really names less an object than a particular subject-object relation". Such thinking is important when thinking about waste management in the context of preventing or safeguarding against the effects of wasting. It indicates a perspective that justifies the intervention of the legislator.

Things only gain "life" to the extent that they serve our purposes. This is another aspect of the relational statute of waste, which can gain another life if its potential is correlated with its purpose. I am in favour of the assertion that "category of waste marks the temporal suspension of utile time rather than time's absolute erasure".[14]

---

[7] Stallabrass (2009),p. 416.

[8] Kennedy (2007), p. 54.

[9] Kennedy (2007), p. 123.

[10] Harman (2002), p. 21.

[11] Viney (2014), p. 37.

[12] Heidegger (1962), p. 104.

[13] Brown (2001).

[14] Viney (2014), p. 16.

This objective does not have to be individual, it can have a social dimension. It requires financial means through which it will be given new life. The financial market, in which money is a commodity, is a mean of acquiring such resources. An element of the financial market is the insurance market. Combining this with the essence of the insurance business, which is the assumption of risks, allows to make an argument that the institutions of insurance law can be used to finance such objectives.

From a methodological standpoint, this inquiry serves a clarifying function: the relativity and indeterminacy of what counts as "waste" directly affect the scope and applicability of legal norms, including those governing insurance mechanisms for ecological risk. If the status of waste is relative—as the text notes—it complicates both the identification of associated risks and the design of appropriate legal and financial safeguards. Thus, conceptual analysis a scientifically necessary step toward delimiting the subject matter of legal regulation.

From an epistemological point of view, philosophical and linguistic analysis places the legal category of waste in the broader context of human experience of materiality and temporality. As scholars such as Mary Douglas and William Viney have shown, waste is defined not by its intrinsic properties, but by its spatial and temporal displacement—it is "matter out of place" and "matter out of time." This approach has direct implications for law: legal classification systems reflect cultural understandings of order, value, and exclusion. Therefore, any legal framework for environmental waste management, including the use of insurance as a risk transfer instrument, must be based on a clear awareness of these fundamental conceptual structures.

From a systemic-legal perspective, insurance law is based on the categorization of risk. Philosophical analysis reveals the inherent temporality and relationality of waste—characteristics that closely correspond to the probabilistic and future-oriented nature of insurance. Both waste and insurance concern value deferred in time: in one case, the deferred potential of discarded materials; in the other, the deferred realization of risk. Recognizing this structural analogy provides a scientifically coherent bridge between philosophical semantics and dogmatic-legal inquiries.

2 Research Objective and Research Methods

Academic work on waste predominantly takes place within the natural sciences and technology, but the number of researchers addressing waste from a humanistic and societal perspective increases in last years.[15] This approach also characterises legal science. Despite the growing interest in waste issues from an environmental law perspective, there is a lack of studies analysing these phenomena from an insurance law perspective.

[15] Ek and Johansson (2020).

Comparative law is influenced by the phenomenon of legal culture clash within the "great dichotomy" of state law and common law observed in the European Union.[16] As a result, differences in law-making and particularly in law application in Member States have gradually disappeared. This process was so advanced that it was not hindered by Brexit. An expression of this trend is the appreciation of precedents—the basis of the common law system, in countries with Germanic and Romance traditions.[17] The task of the Court of Justice is to ensure that the law is respected in the process of interpretation and application. It has therefore been of particular interest in the research of the legal principles supporting the use of insurance for waste management. Member States were obliged to establish measures necessary to ensure effective legal protection in areas covered by EU law (Article 19(1) TFEU). The Court of Justice relies on national courts which have become co-responsible for the enforcement of EU law.[18] Hence the interest in this paper in the case law of national courts fulfilling the EU mission. The monograph also takes into account the traditional division of legal orders into civil law legal cultures, distinguishing the Romance and Germanic circles, and common law. The disproportion in the volume of the sections devoted to the individual models is due to the differences in the doctrinal achievements of the individual legal orders and the significance of the concepts developed from the point of view of the considerations included in the monograph. The comparative legal analysis essentially concerned the legal solutions adopted in the individual Member States. The clarity of the argument, the leading role of the national legal systems and the novelty of the solutions were the criteria for selecting the solutions to be compared. Due to the maturity of the US insurance market translating into the development of insurance law, the legal solutions used there were also analysed. An additional argument for choosing the United States as a reference point for the analysis of European solutions was the regionalism of the two legal orders, EU and state, facilitating comparison.

The study focuses on waste which poses a risk to the environment and can consequently be the subject of insurance coverage. Municipal waste represents about 10% of the total waste generated in the EU, but it is one of the most complex waste streams to manage due to its diverse composition, the large number of waste producers and the fragmentation of responsibilities for its management. However, due to the fact that they are treated as waste managed within public services (by municipality authorities), it's challenging to treat them as an insurance risk due to the difficulty in indicating an insurable interest. Biowaste is the most important municipal waste stream, since it constitutes on average 34% of municipal waste. Sound biowaste management could enable its use as a fertiliser and soil improver and for the production of biogas. Author's failure to undertake research on biowaste is precisely because of its potential beneficial impact on the environment.

[16] Tokarczyk (2005), p. 154.

[17] Zirk-Sadowski (2000), p. 9 et seq.

[18] Prechal (2005), p. 184 et seq.

The main research problem concerned establishing the role of insurance in waste management. The thesis that insurance is an instrument of rational, ecological waste management was verified. The terms "rational" and "ecological" are integral to waste management discourse, emphasizing efficiency and environmental sustainability, respectively. Rationality is understood as an efficient and well-organized approach to waste management. In the spirit of EU law, efficient use of resources and minimization of waste generation requires rational planning and management strategies. Ecological aspect underscores environmental protection by advocating for waste management practices that prevent harm to human health and the environment. Due to the specificity of insurance as both economic and legal category and the influence of economic sciences on EU law, the study includes considerations of an economic nature. Their character is subsidiary to the legal perspective dominating the paper.

The carried out dogmatic-legal, functional and legal comparative analyses were aimed at answering the question: can, and if so, in what form can insurance activities support waste management? This research problem determined the structure of the monograph, channeling it to thinking in insurance terms while taking into account the specificities of waste management.

3 Structure and Detailed Research Questions

The results of the analysis have been presented in five chapters (2–6).

Therefore, it became essential to identify the insurance risks associated with waste management called waste risks in the paper (two chapter). The starting point was the concept of waste and the reference to the product. In order to establish the scope of the term "waste," it is necessary to clarify the term "by-product," which, like waste, belongs to the broader group of residues. Another question was to establish the relevance of the waste classification to the studied issue, the type of waste management and the relevance of the type of waste and its management. The research was aimed at verifying the thesis that determination whether one is dealing with waste and if so—what type of waste and what its management is, has an impact on the requirement for financial security and the choice of insurance as such security.

The main objective determined the selection of legal principles that can support the use of insurance in waste management (three chapter). Four principles shaped by EU law were indicated, which was important given the primary focus of the research. .However, the significance of two of them is not limited to EU or European law. The question was raised: to what extent do the principles of prevention and precaution, which are key to environmental law, strengthen the preventive function in waste insurance? Furthermore, to what extent are these findings consistent with the paradigm shift from risk transfer to risk prevention? To answer this question, it was necessary to clarify the conceptual scope of both principles and relate them to the issue at hand. The "polluter pays" principle was recognized as another guiding principle in the development of waste insurance, and in relation to waste management, it was clarified as the "possessor pays" principle. This study attempts to answer the question of whether the designation of the waste holder as the entity responsible for the negative impact of waste management on the environment is reflected in legal regulations. This is important from the point of view of the subjective scope of another of the principles analyzed: the principle of extended producer responsibility (EPR). Unlike the "polluter pays" principle, the EPR principle focuses on the entire life cycle of a product, including the phase in which it becomes waste, rather than on the harmful impact of production and consumption. It was necessary to assess the extent to which the responsibility of the waste producer is consistent with the financial and/or organizational obligations related to waste management. The concept of the product life cycle seems to be consistent with the principles of the circular economy model. The idea of Environmental Social Governance sets the direction for the development of EU law. The question arises as to what extent it helps to identify the entities and scope of responsibility for the environmentally harmful effects of waste management. In the pursuit of legal solutions pertaining to the financial liability for deleterious environmental effects associated with waste management, a meticulous examination was conducted of EU regulations on financial security. An attempt was made to answer the question of how far the legislator's intervention extends and how mandatory financial security should be understood. In this regard, a comparative analysis was conducted between EU solutions and those adopted in the US. This issue gave rise to a confrontation between financial security and the principle of limited liability. In the context of the dissertation's primary objective, the central inquiry pertained to the extent to which insurance activities could be considered as forms of financial security. Another question concerned the extent of the legislator's interference in the way waste management claims are secured by insurance. The present study seeks to ascertain whether the manner in which waste is managed, or the nature of the waste itself, exerts an influence on the response to the aforementioned question.

The considerations in four chapter are an attempt to assess the extent of the legislator's interference in various types of waste management posing an environmental risk. It involved pointing out the importance of more specific issues such as the entity determining the amount of security. To provide a comprehensive response to the question of using insurance as a financial security measure, we must delve into the legal intricacies of financial security, particularly its status as personal security. Identifying insurance with an insurance contract has led this chapter to focus on the insurance contract as a type of financial security. A comparison has therefore been made between the insurance contract and other forms of financial security, with the aim of answering the question of whether the insurance contract is the most suitable form of financial security for supporting ecological waste management and, if so, to what extent. A significant place in the paper is devoted to the second insurance activity—the insurance guarantee, and its relevance to waste management risks. Two considerations justify the need to address this topic in a separate and comprehensive manner. First, the institution of the insurance guarantee remains largely overlooked in the academic literature, despite its increasing functional importance in practice. Second, this instrument is already used on the insurance market to secure environmental obligations related to waste, yet its legal nature, structural characteristics and relationship to other security mechanisms have not been sufficiently clarified. The lack of regulations governing insurance guarantees necessitated a more in-depth analysis of the legal nature of guarantee insurance in relation to legal cultures, as well as answers to questions concerning the origin of this legal act and its position within contract law. This led to an examination of the similarities and differences between guarantee insurance and other guarantee contracts. The next question concerned the structure of guarantee insurance, essentially asking whether it constitutes a tripartite relationship. Attempting to answer the question of which characteristics define guarantee insurance required a comparison with institutions performing similar security functions, such as suretyship, deposits and insurance contracts. Given the dissertation's primary objective, it is crucial to determine which differences between these institutions are significant when they are used as financial security by waste holders.

The final six chapter attempts to verify the adequacy of the insurance solutions operating in the insurance market to meet waste management needs. Therefore, an attempt was made to answer the question of the extent to which the waste risks identified in Chapter 1 constitute insurable risks, and to define insurable interest in waste insurance. Starting with an analysis of traditional civil liability insurance, the question was raised as to the extent to which it provides insurance protection in the event of environmental damage related to waste management. The next question is whether environmental liability insurance can be used to implement environmentally sound waste management. Do the barriers inherent in third-party insurance also exist in the case of first-party insurance, particularly environmental cost insurance? To what extent does this type of insurance protect against waste-related risks?. Alongside the analysis of insurance conditions and case law shaping insurance law, attention was paid to the issue of waste insurance distribution. The social function of the insurance under study influences their specificity expressed in the role of authority. This raises the question of the place of authority in the insurance relationship formation.

References

Brown B (2001) Thing theory. Crit Inq 28(1)

Douglas M (2002) Purity and danger: an analysis of concepts of pollution and Taboo, first published 1966. Routledge, Abingdon

Ek R, Johansson N (2020) Perspective on waste from the social sciences and humanities. Cambridge Scholars Publishing

Harman G (2002) Tool-being: Heidegger and the metaphysics of objects. Open Court, Chicago

Heidegger M (1962) Being and Time (trans: John Macquarrie and Edward Robinson). Blackwell, Oxford

Kennedy G (2007) An ontology of trash: the disposable and its problematic nature. State University of New York Press, Albany

Laffont J-J (2008) Externalities. In: Blume LE, Durlauf SN (eds) The new Palgrave dictionary of economics, 2nd edn. Palgrave Macmillan

Prechal S (2005) Directives in European law. Oxford University Press
Rogers H (2006) Gone tomorrow: the hidden life of Garbage. September 2006
Stallabrass J (2009) Trash. In: Candlin F, Guins R (eds) The object reader. Routledge, London
Strasser S (1999) Waste and want: a social history of trash. Owl Books, New York
Tokarczyk R (2005) Komparatystyka prawnicza, Kraków
Viney W (2014) Waste. A philosophy of things. Bloomsbury Publishing
Zirk-Sadowski M (2000) Wprowadzenie do filozofii prawa. Kraków

Waste Risks

1 Introduction

From the perspective of the primary research objective, the fundamental issue is to ascertain the scope of waste risks that would be covered by insurance. In order to proceed with the present undertaking, it is first necessary to define the concept of waste from a legal perspective. The dissertation's primary focus was on EU law, which exerts a substantial influence on the national legislation of Member States by regulating waste management.

In order to provide an answer to the question of what constitutes waste and what does not, a comparison of waste to a product was necessary. It is therefore imperative to initiate a search for the conclusion of the product, in addition to elucidating the notion of by-product. It is evident that by-products, similar to waste, fall within the overarching category of residues. A further issue that had to be resolved was to ascertain the significance of waste classification for the subject under study. It is important to note that not all waste poses an equal threat to the environment. This underscores the necessity for the effective management of hazardous waste.

In order to establish a robust framework for environmental protection, it is imperative to ascertain the extent to which waste risks are concomitant with environmental risks. Pollution (emissions causing specific negative consequences) is materialisation of environmental risk.The concept of environmental damage can be defined as the materialisation of environmental risk, and simultaneously, the condition for the liability of the perpetrator, as well as that of the insurer. Therefore, considerations devoted to environmental damage are constituted as the materialisation of waste risk.

The issue of waste risk is most clearly demonstrated in the context of waste management. It is important to note that not all forms of waste management are equally significant from the perspective of waste risk. Therefore, it is essential to examine how the EU classification affects the definition of the area of waste management

D. Maśniak, *The Legal Framework for the Use of Insurance in Ecological Waste Management*, AIDA Europe Research Series on Insurance Law and Regulation 17, https://doi.org/10.1007/978-3-032-26550-0_2

that is relevant from the point of view of insurance coverage. The intervention of the EU legislator in the EU is specific and differs from the solutions adopted on other continents. To illustrate this, legal solutions concerning waste management in the US are indicated.

Webster's Third New International Dictionary defines 'waste' as 'damaged, defective or superfluous material produced during or left over from a manufacturing process or industrial operation; material not usable for the ordinary or main purpose of manufacture'. As an example of such 'waste', the dictionary mentions "material rejected during a textile manufacturing process and either recovered for reworking (as yarn) or used usually for wiping dirt and oil from hands and machinery.[1]

2 The Concept of Waste in the EU

2.1 Definition of Waste

The EU law adopts a very general definition linking waste with the decision of the holder to discard it. According to the definition adopted in the Waste Directive[2] and used in the entire EU waste management legislation, 'waste' means any substance or object which the holder discards or intends or is required to discard. The legislator refrained from presenting a waste catalogue (Article 3 (1) of the Directive), leaving such a catalog for a separate category of 'hazardous waste' (Article 3 (2) of the Directive).

The definition of waste based on the act of discarding rather than the value of the material could be problematic. Unfortunately, it is not clear what is meant by discarding. This definition corresponds to the changing reality, where waste streams become more and more problematic due to the variety and complexity of all new products available on the market, especially in the electric and electronic field.

The case law of the European Court of Justice (CJEU) which has opted to emphasize the environmental aspects of the Waste Directive is of fundamental importance for the comprehension of the notion of waste. The Court has adopted a case-by-case approach, considering all the factual circumstances involved.[3] That means that, for

---

[1] Webster's Third New International Dictionary of the English Language, Unabridged (Springfield, MA: G. & C. Merriam Company, 1961), s.v. "waste."

[2] Directive 2008/98/EC of the European Parliament and of the Council of 19 November 2008 on waste and repealing certain Directives (Text with EEA relevance) OJ L 312, 22.11.2008, pp. 3–30 hereafter designated as the Waste Directive.

[3] Given that in 2008 the EU avoided the issues by including an exception as Article 2(1)(b) in the revised Waste Framework Directive for "land (in situ) including unexcavated contaminated soil and buildings permanently connected with land", some European Court of Justice rulings became out of date, e.g. Case C-1/03 *Van de Walle v Texaco Belgium SA* [2004] ECR I-7613, paragraphs 47–50; https://eur-lex.europa.eu/legal-content/EN/TXT/?uri=CELEX%3A62003CJ0001 that concerned considering unexcavated contaminated soil as waste.

that general rule to be applied, the elements characterising the intent of a holder of waste must be taken into account. According to case-law, classifying a substance or an object as waste can be inferred primarily from the holder's actions and the meaning of the term 'discard'. The Court has defined relevant criteria for the purposes of determining whether a substance or an object, including materials, is to be considered waste. As regards the meaning of the term 'discard', it also follows from the Court's case-law that this term must be interpreted in the light of the aim of Waste Directive. According to recital 6 thereof, the purpose is to minimise the negative effects of waste's generation and management on human health and the environment, considering Article 191(2) TFUE which provides that the EU environmental policy is to aim at a high level of protection and is to be based, in particular, on the precautionary principle and preventive actions(as discussed in more detail below). It follows that the term 'discard', and therefore the concept of 'waste' cannot be interpreted restrictively.[4] Within the meaning of points 15 and 19 of Article 3 of that directive,[5] the term 'discard' covers both 'recovery' and 'disposal' of a substance or an object. More precisely, the existence of 'waste must be determined in the light of all the circumstances, taking into account the purpose of that directive and the need to ensure that its effectiveness is not undermined. Thus, certain circumstances may demonstrate that a substance or an object has been discarded or there was some intent or requirement to discard it within the meaning of point 1 of Article 3 of Waste Directive,[6] for example a fact that a substance is a production or consumption residue, that is to say, a product which was not itself sought.[7] According to the Court, it is about the fact that the substance or object in question is not or is no longer of any use to its holder, such that that substance or object constitutes a burden which that holder will seek to discard.[8] Furthermore, neither the method used to treat a substance nor the use to which it is put will conclusively determine whether or not the substance is classified as "waste". Finally, the concept of "waste" does not exclude either substances or objects that are capable of being re-used in an economic sense.[9] Such evidence may likewise be constituted by the fact that the substance in question is a production residue for which special precautions must be taken if it is used owing to the environmentally hazardous nature of its composition.[10]

---

[4] Judgment of 4 July 2019, *Tronex*, C-624/17, EU:C:2019:564, paragraph 18 and the case-law cited.

[5] Judgment of 4 July 2019, *Tronex*, C-624/17, EU:C:2019:564, paragraph 19 and the case-law cited.

[6] Judgment of 4 July 2019, *Tronex*, C-624/17, EU:C:2019:564, paragraphs 20 and 21.

[7] See judgments of 24 June 2008, *Commune de Mesquer*, C-188/07, EU:C:2008:359, paragraph 41, and of 3 October 2013, *Brady*, C-113/12, EU:C:2013:627, paragraph 40.

[8] Judgment of 4 July 2019, Tronex C-624/17, EU:C:2019:564, paragraph 22 and the case-law cited.

[9] Judgment of 3 October 2013, Brady C-113/12, EU:C:2013:627, paragraph 42 and the case-law cited.

[10] judgment of 3 October 2013, *Brady*, C-113/12, EU:C:2013:627, paragraph 41 and the case-law cited.

In the case of Commune de Mesquer v Total France SA, the CJEU was asked to rule on whether hydrocarbon spills are waste. The case concerned Erika, a small tanker that broke in two in rough seas on December 12, 1999 around 35 nautical miles from the coast of Brittany in France's exclusive economic zone, spilling 19,800 tonnes of heavy fuel oil. The fuel oil belonged to Total France SA that sold it to Total International Ltd. which then contracted with ENEL, a large Italian energy company, to transport the oil to Sicily. Both Total companies eventually paid more than €200 million for the remediation of the oil waste that contaminated around 400 kilometres of coast, killing more than 75,000 birds and other wildlife. The municipality of Mesquer, whose coastline had been heavily polluted by oil, has carried out clean-up operations. The municipality filed a lawsuit to the Commercial Court of Saint-Hazaire, claiming reimbursement from Total. The action was dismissed, as was an appeal to the Rennes Court of Appeal. Under French law crude oil was considered a *commercial product*, not waste, so the producer or seller (Total) was not held liable.Following another appeal, the court of cassation debated whether the hydrocarbon spills that were accidentally spilled at sea by the wrecked tanker, then mixed with water and sediment before being dumped on the French coast were in fact waste. The legal problem arose because after the oil spill, the oil became an unusable substance requiring disposal—meaning it *could* be considered "waste" under EU law.[11] French law, however, interpreted that concept more narrowly, excluding such cases from producer liability. The CJEU ruled that the hydrocarbon spills were waste within the meaning of the Waste Directive. Furthermore, CJEU's position was that Total France was the waste holder because it was its possessor and producer.The court further ruled that Total International could be liable as an original producer or former waste holder if it 'contributed by [its] conduct to the risk that the pollution caused by the shipwreck [would] occur'.[12] The CJEU also pointed out the close connection between liability under the Waste Framework Directive and liability for waste disposal.

2.2 *Waste Versus by-Product*

The product-waste relationship causes a significant problem. There are difficulties in distinguishing waste from by-products that are not treated as waste under EU waste law. A production residue ("a substance or object, resulting from a production process, the primary aim of which is not the production of that item") that fulfils the conditions of Article 5(1) of Waste Directive is a by-product only if the following

[11] When the Erika disaster occurred (1999) and when the case was brought before the CJEU (2007), Directive 75/442/EEC (amended by 91/156/EEC) was still in force. This was the first EU-wide legal framework establishing common rules for waste management, hereinafter referred to as the Waste Framework Directive.

[12] Case C-188/07 *Commune de Mesquer v Total France SA* [2008] ECR I-4501, paragraphs 57–59; https://curia.europa.eu/juris/liste.jsf?language=en&num=C-188/07.

conditions are met: a. further use of the substance or object is certain; b. the substance or object can be used directly without any further processing other than normal industrial practice; c. the substance or object is produced as an integral part of a production process; and d. further use is lawful. It has to be decided on a case by case basis.

The guidance on how to interpret the first of these conditions (a.) can be found in the Brady judgment. By interpreting Directive 75/442 (Waste Framework Directive), the Court recognized that slurry produced in farms as a secondary product and sold to other farmers for reuse as fertiliser could be regarded as a by-product.[13] Primarily, the farmers' plots of land where the material is to be supplied must be clearly identified from the outset. Next, the material must actually be intended to be reused, and the quantity is to be strictly limited to the needs of the established use. Futher, the supply of the material must actually be used or marketed on terms that are economically advantageous to its holder. Also, in case the slurry at issue is not supplied immediately, it's obligatory to use appropriate and sufficient storage to prevent the soil from contamination during the period of storage. Moreover, the storage duration must not exceed what is required in order for the undertaking to be able to meet its contractual commitments.[14] The Court of Justice has now clarified how the condition that the further use of a substance or object must be certain should be understood.

Article 5(1)(b) of Waste Directive sets out a condition that it must be possible to use the substance or object directly without further processing other than normal industrial practice (b). An example of this is excavated materials, classified in case 238/21.[15] The CJEU recognised that the condition is fulfilled if the excavated materials were subject to a quality control proving that they are uncontaminated materials in the highest quality class and are recognised as such under national law. However, the Court emphasized that the referring court should ensure that the materials did not require any processing or treatment before further use.

With regard to the third condition (c), according to which the substance or object must be produced as an integral part of a production process, Advocate General in case C- 238/21 made some interesting reflections about excavated soil used for the levelling of land. He claims that the term 'production process' should be interpreted as encompassing economic transformation activities that go beyond those that take place exclusively within an industrial context. Excavated soil is the inevitable result of one of the first steps usually undertaken in a construction operation as an economic activity, the result of which is the transformation of land. For that reason, excavated soil should be regarded as an integral part of a production process.[16]

---

[13] See Judgment of 3 October 2013, Brady C-113/12, EU:C:2013:627, paragraph 60.

[14] Judgment of 3 October 2013, Brady C-113/12, EU:C:2013:627, paragraph 53, 54, 55, 56.

[15] Case 238/21 Porr Bau GmbH v. Bezirkshauptmannschaft Graz-Umgebung ECLI:EU:C:2022:885.

[16] Opinion of Advocate General Medina delivered on 22 June 2022(1); Case C-238/21 Porr Bau GmbH v.

Bezirkshauptmannschaft Graz-Umgebung, paragraph 47–48.

Finally, as regards the legality requirement of the continued use of a substance or object, Article 5(1)(d) of Waste Directive requires, in particular, that the substance or object fulfils all relevant product, environmental and health requirements relating to its specific use and does not result in overall adverse environmental or human health impacts. An example is the classification of excavated soil, both in terms of it being non-polluting and its suitability for a specific land adaptation purpose, based on a quality analysis carried out prior to its re-use, as the highest quality unpolluted material.[17]

Article 5(1) of Waste Directive[18] in essence, refers to a substance or object which the holder is not willing to discard, due to the financial advantage that might be obtained from its reuse, and which cannot therefore be regarded as a burden and thus as a waste. In the Court's view, it would not be justified to make a substance or object which the holder intends to exploit or market on economically advantageous terms, within a subsequent recovery process, subject to the strict requirements of Waste Directive on environment and human health protection.[19] Thus, distinguishing waste from by-product boils down to deciding whether the holder of the materials intends to discard them, resulting in waste, or to use them in an economically beneficial way, resulting in a by-product.[20]

2.3 Waste as a Residue

The waste hierarchy enounced in Article 4 of the Waste Directive indicates the preferred options in waste handling, because they deliver the best environmental outcome. The order of priority is as follows: prevention, preparing for reuse, recycling, other recovery (e.g. energy recovery) and disposal in landfills. It closes the loop between product and waste by introducing the concept of life cycle thinking. As demonstrated in Fig. 1, both products and waste are classified within a broader category of residues, and the distinction between them (the end of waste status) is not clearly delineated.

In order for waste to achieve the status of "end of waste" (as Fig. 1 shows), it is necessary that it serves a useful purpose by substituting other materials. This constitutes the essence of a recovery operation. The Court of Justice of the European Union (CJEU), through a number of judgments, has provided guidance on when a

---

[17] Opinion of Advocate General Medina delivered on 22 June 2022(1); Case C-238/21 Porr Bau GmbH v.

Bezirkshauptmannschaft Graz-Umgebung paragraph 49–51.

[18] The case-law is at the heart of the concept of 'by-product', which was subsequently codified in Article 5(1) of Directive 2008/98. Instead of the term 'extraction or manufacturing process', the term 'production process' was used—see, inter alia, the judgment in *Sappi*, paragraph 51 and the case-law cited.

[19] Judgment of 4 July 2019, Tronex C-624/17, EU:C:2019:564, paragraph 24 and the case-law cited.

[20] Judgment in *Sappi*, paragraph 53 and the case-law cited.

material can be regarded as something an undertaking seeks to exploit, rather than as a substance or object which is being discarded. According to Article 6 of the Waste Framework Directive, waste may cease to be waste following a recovery operation, provided that the following cumulative conditions are fulfilled: 1. the substance or object is commonly used for specific purposes; 2. there is a market or demand for such a substance or object; 3. the substance or object fulfils the technical requirements for its specific purpose and meets the existing legislation and standards applicable to products; 4. the use of the substance or object will not lead to overall adverse environmental or human-health impacts.[21] These four conditions are of a factual and technical nature, as they concern the material characteristics, quality and practical usability of the recovered substance.

At the legal level, the CJEU has further clarified how these factual criteria interact with the discretion of Member States in determining when waste may cease to be waste. In its Tallinna Vesi judgment,[22] the Court examined whether, in the absence of harmonised Union-level criteria, a Member State is obliged to recognise the end-of-waste status once the factual conditions under Article 6 are met. The Court held that the EU legislature has not defined the precise nature of measures governing the end-of-waste status and, consequently, that Member States retain a degree of discretion to adopt generally applicable rules or to make case-by-case assessments. Importantly, the Tallinna Vesi ruling also confirmed that the mere fulfilment of the material conditions set out in Article 6(1) does not automatically entail recognition of the end-of-waste status. National authorities are entitled to consider broader environmental and health-related factors—such as the potential presence of hazardous

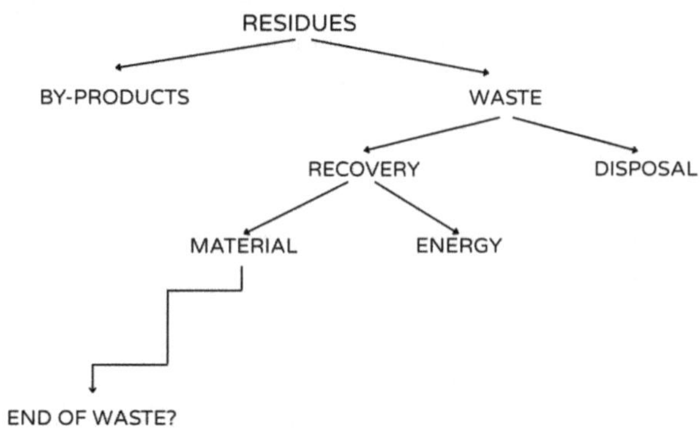

Fig. 1 Classification of residues. Source: Clelia Antico, Environmental Implementation DG Environment, European Commision. https://www.eracomm.eu/combatting_waste_crime/speakers_contributions/1_Antico_overview.pdf

[21] There is an important link between the end of waste criteria and Regulation (EC) No 1907/2006), i. e the EU regulation on chemical substances. As emphasized by the Waste Directive Guidelines issued by the Commission in 2012 (https://ec.europa.eu/environment/waste/framework/pdf/guidance_doc.pdf), whomever places the material on the market for the first time after it has achieved the "end of waste" status must ensure that the material meets the relevant requirements under applicable products regulation.

[22] Court of Justice, judgment of 28 March 2019, AS Tallinna Vesi v Keskkonnaamet, C-60/18, EU:C:2019:264.

substances—and may, on that basis, refuse to grant EoW status to particular waste streams, as was the case with sewage sludge in Tallinna Vesi.

Thus, the Tallinna Vesi case concerns both the substantive interpretation of the material criteria and the legal framework within which Member States exercise their discretion. Nevertheless, Member States must ensure that their national legislation, or the absence thereof, does not hinder the attainment of the objectives of the Waste Framework Directive. As established by the Court, these objectives include promoting the application of the waste hierarchy (Article 4 of the Directive) and, as emphasised in recitals 8 and 29, encouraging waste recovery and the use of recovered materials in order to conserve natural resources and foster the development of a circular economy.[23]

2.4 *Hazardous Waste*

Due to their environmental impact, hazardous waste are considered special subgroups of waste and are distinguished by their particularly negative impact. The EU legislator defines them by the hazardous properties listed in Annex III of the Waste Directive. Waste is considered hazardous if it has one or more hazardous properties. This legal solution significantly expands the scope of waste treated as hazardous.

The classification of waste as hazardous or non-hazardous, and in particular understanding when and under what circumstances waste is to be considered hazardous, is a crucial decision in the entire waste management chain from generation to final treatment. Correct classification of waste as hazardous triggers a number of important obligations, for example in terms of labelling and packaging, but also in terms of the available compliant treatment.[24]

There is a strict specification in EU law „in order to prevent or limit, as far as possible, the potential negative effects on the environment and on human health due to inappropriate management"(recital 14 of the Preamble to The Waste Directive). In order to encourage a harmonized classification of waste and ensure the harmonized determination of hazardous waste within the Community waste and hazardous waste have been classified in accordance with the list of the types of waste as last established by Commission Decision 2000/532/EU.[25] Member States should encourage the separation of hazardous compounds from waste streams if necessary to achieve environmentally sound management. (recital 28 of the Preamble to the Waste Directive). According to Art. 7.1. of the Waste Directive, "the inclusion of a substance or object in the list shall not mean that it is waste in all circumstances".

---

[23] See judgment of 3 October 2013, Brady C-113/12, EU:C:2013:627, paragraph 52–56.

[24] Commission notice on technical guidance on the classification of waste (2018/C 124/01).

[25] Decision 2000/532/EC of 3 May 2000 replacing Decision 94/3/EC establishing a list of wastes pursuant to Article 1(a) of Council Directive 75/442/EEC on waste and Council Decision 94/904/EC establishing a list of hazardous waste pursuant to Article 1(4) of Council Directive 91/689/EEC on hazardous waste (OJ L 226, 6.9.2000, p. 3).

The EU legislator emphasized that hazardous waste is a subgroup of waste, that is, qualifying it as waste requires having the properties referred to in Art. 3.1. A Member State may consider waste as hazardous even if it does not appear on the list of waste, but it displays one or more of the properties listed in Annex III to the Waste Directive. The list shall take into account the origin and composition of the waste and, where necessary, limit values of concentration. On the other hand, "where a Member State has evidence to show that specific waste that appears on the list as hazardous waste does not display any of the properties listed in Annex III, it may consider that waste as non-hazardous waste" (Art. 7 of the Waste Directive).

The control of the hazardous waste management is achieved by using the ban on the mixing of hazardous waste. According to this principle, the "hazardous waste is not mixed, either with other categories of hazardous waste or with other waste, substances or materials. Mixing shall include the dilution of hazardous substances" (Art. 18 of the Waste Directive). This prohibition is also the basis of the waste disposal legislation.

There is a question about the impact the ban has on mixing of hazardous waste on insurance coverage. Although hazardous waste management appears to be of higher risk by its nature, the risk may turn out to be more insurable than other waste management risks. This is due to the greater influence of the legislator in this area, which influences the clarification of requirements that translates into risk estimation. The specific financial safeguards imposed by the legislator (discussed in more detail below) also play a non-negligible role.

According to the provisions of the Landfill Directive, hazardous waste should be disposed of on separate landfills (Art. 4 of the Landfill Directive). This solution affects the risk assessment of hazardous waste storage. On the one hand, it facilitates such an assessment by specifying the waste, on the other hand, it constitutes a risk that is difficult to accept for the insurer due to the high probability of environmental damages caused by hazardous waste management.

3 Waste Management in EU: Classification

Back in 1997, the Council of the European Union in its resolution[26] confirmed that "waste prevention should be the first priority of waste management, and that re-use and material recycling should be preferred to energy recovery from waste" (recital 7 of the Waste Directive). This recognizes the very broad understanding of the concept of waste management and links it with the waste hierarchy mentioned above (Art. 4 Waste Directive). Focusing on the environmental impacts of waste generation and management throughout the resources life cycle is part of the environmental protection objectives set out in Article 191 of the Treaty on the Functioning of

[26] Resolution of 24 February 1997 on a Community strategy for waste management OJ C 76, 11.3.1997, p. 1.

the European Union, which include "reasonable and rational use of natural resources".

The Fig. 2 illustrates the types of operations covered by the concept of waste management under EU waste law.

Such a broad approach to the concept of waste management, related to the waste hierarchy, results in a different degree of environmental impact of individual types of operations. Some of them (such as landfilling or incineration) are recognized as significant threats to humans and the environment, and others (such as recycling) as preferred forms of waste management from the environmental protection point of view of. This means that the various insurance needs will be generated by risks associated with each type of waste management.

The EU legislator defines collection as "gathering of waste, including the preliminary sorting and preliminary storage of waste for the purposes of transport to a waste treatment facility" (Article 3 point 10 of the Waste Directive).

Recovery "means any operation the principal result of which is waste serving a useful purpose by replacing other materials which would otherwise have been used to fulfil a particular function, or waste being prepared to fulfil that function, in the plant or in the wider economy" (Articel 3 point 15 of the Waste Directive).

Recycling was distinguished as a special type of recovery "by which waste materials are reprocessed into products, materials or substances whether for the original or other purposes. It includes the reprocessing of organic material but does not include energy recovery and the reprocessing into materials that are to be used as fuels or for backfilling operations" (Article 3 point 17 of the Waste Directive). Whereas disposal "means any operation which is not recovery even where the operation has as a secondary consequence the reclamation of substances or energy" (Article 3 point 19 of the Waste Directive).

In comparison to the types of disposal mentioned below, recycling is characterized by a positive impact on the environment. It saves energy, because generally less energy is required to manufacture products from recycled feedstocks and hence the emissions of pollutants is lower. Recycling process prolongs the reserves of finite resources (e.g. metal ores) and contributes to the sustainable use of resources. Just as importantly, it limits the impacts associated with extraction of virgin raw material (e.g. quarrying of ores and sand, felling of old growth forests to produce wood for

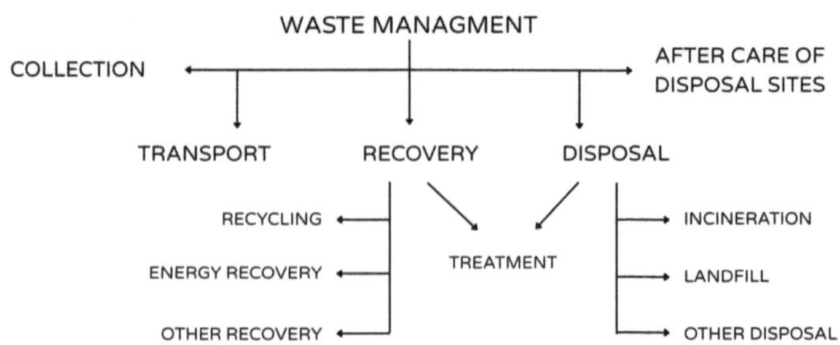

Fig. 2 Waste Management-Types of Operations. Source: own study

paper).[27] So-called recycling insurance, which takes into account the specificity of such activities, can be an answer to such activities.

Disposal "means any operation which is not recovery even where the operation has as a secondary consequence the reclamation of substances or energy" (Aritcle 3 point 19 of the Waste Directive).

Landfilling, classified the lowest in the waste disposal hierarchy, generates such environmental risks as: methane emissions from biodegradable waste contributing to global warming and local hazards such as the risk of fires and explosions, risks of water pollution from leachate formed during waste decomposition, non-sustainable use of land, noise and odor harming human and animals life. Also, some carbon compounds may be retained in the landfill for long periods (sequestered) and so are not returned to the atmosphere as CO2. Incineration (as another type of disposal) generates the following risks: emissions of harmful air pollutants such as NOx, SO2, HCl, fine particles and dioxin, emissions of carbon dioxide from fossil waste (e.g. plastics) and N2O contributing to global warming, fly ash and air pollution control residues which then require stabilization and disposal as hazardous waste.

At the same time, however, incineration is a more preferred form of waste management, which places it higher than landfill in the waste hierarchy. Energy recovered from incineration can replace fossil fuels that helps avoid carbon dioxide emissions. Bottom ash can be reused as secondary aggregate, and metals can be recycled from bottom ash.

4 Waste Management in the U.S.

4.1 Statutory Law-Permitting

Federal and state authorities can require those who have stored waste without a permit or in violation of its conditions to remove the waste and clean up the contamination. The main federal environmental permitting laws relevant to the discussion of waste insurance are the Resource Conservation and Recovery Act (RCRA)[28] which regulates the handling, treatment, storage, disposal and transportation of non-hazardous and hazardous waste, and the Clean Water Act (CWA),[29] which regulates the discharge of pollutants into the U.S. waters.

The CWA and RCRA are implemented by the federal government and the states in accordance with cooperative federalism. Under this system, the U.S. Environmental Protection Agency (EPA) has regulatory, oversight and enforcement responsibilities. When federal law and/or EPA regulations are changed, the state must update its plan to reflect the changes and seek EPA's approval of the updated plan for

[27] Smith (2001), p. 19 https://ec.europa.eu/environment/pdf/waste/studies/climate_change.pdf.

[28] 42 United States Code paragraph 6901 *et seq.*

[29] 33 United States Code paragraph 1251 *et seq.*

implementation and enforcement. RCRA established a framework for managing hazardous and non-hazardous waste. RCRA requires, among other things, that a company or a person that generates hazardous waste above a certain threshold or that transports hazardous waste obtains a generator identification number (RCRA Site ID) from the EPA. RCRA also requires owners and operators of treatment, storage and disposal facilities (TSDFs) to obtain a RCRA Site ID number and a permit to operate the facility. The hazardous waste program operates under cooperative federalism. The states play a leading role in regulating underground storage tanks in accordance with RCRA under this system. The states also play a leading role in implementing non-hazardous waste programs, including waste disposal facilities.

4.2 Superfund

The CERCLA Law, passed by the U.S. Congress on December 11.1980, is the way to solve the problem of historically contaminated sites cleanup is. Subsequently, states passed their own mini-CERCLA laws. The Love Canal case in Niagara Falls, New York, where a school was built over a dumpsite containing some 25,000 tons of chemical waste, became the impetus for these laws.

CERCLA has established a national program called Superfund to clean up contaminated sites. When the EPA discovers or is notified that a contaminated site may pose a serious threat to human health or the environment, the contamination at the site is investigated and evaluated to determine whether it should be remediated. Sites that receive a certain high score may be placed on the National Priority List (NPL), a list of the most seriously contaminated sites in the U.S. The NPL, which is implemented and enforced by the EPA, includes federal and non-federal sites. Federal facilities are sites that are owned and/or operated by a U.S. department, agency or another authority. Other facilities are non-federal facilities. There are two types of cleanup measures (called "remedial actions"): (usually long-term measures) and removal actions (short-term measures).

The number of historically contaminated sites turned out to be much larger than the Congress anticipated when, under CERCLA, it established the Hazardous Substances Response Trust Fund, generally known as Superfund, as a revolving fund to implement and enforce the Superfund program. The trust fund was initially established at $1.6 billion (€1,596,168,000) for 5 years in 1980.[30] In 1986, after recognizing the large scale of the program, Congress reauthorized the trust fund at $8.5 billion (€8,480,025,000) for 5 years as part of a broad revision of CERCLA by the Superfund Amendments and Reauthorization Act (SARA). In 1986, the U.S. Congress abolished the trust fund and various dedicated taxes that had been established to fund it. Since then, the Congress has funded the Superfund program with annual appropriations to the EPA. The discontinuation of the trust fund, how-

[30] 42 United States Code paragraph9631(a) (repealed).

ever, does not mean that all contaminated sites, including those on the NPL list, have been cleaned up and that no more seriously contaminated sites have been discovered. As of 3 July 2025, there were 1343 sites on the national priorities list (NPL) of which 1186 were non-federal and 157 were federal. A total of 459 sites had been deleted from the NPL, of which 441 were non-federal and 18 were federal; there was a total of 38 proposed sites, of which 36 were non-federal and 2 were federal.[31]

4.3 Liability Under CERCLA

Liability under CERCLA is strict, joint and several, and retroactive. There are no financial limits on liability for cleanup costs. From a waste management perspective, CERCLA is relevant because liability for cleanup costs applies to the site, which is a "facility"[32] from which there has been a "release" or threat of release of a "hazardous substance"[33] into the "environment". The term "facility" includes any area where a hazardous substance is present, including hazardous waste sites. The term "release" is broadly defined as: "any spilling, leaking, pumping, pouring, emitting, emptying, discharging, injecting, escaping, leaching, dumping, or disposing into the environment (including the abandonment or discarding of barrels, containers, and other closed receptacles containing any hazardous substance or pollutant or contaminant)".

The person liable for the cleanup costs is referred to as the "potentially responsible party" (PRP). PRPs may be: 1. owners or operators of the facility; 2. owners and operators of the facility at the time of "disposal" of the hazardous substance; 3. persons who arranged for the disposal or treatment of the hazardous substance at the facility; and 4. persons who transported the hazardous substance to a facility selected by them. The term "disposal" is defined as: "the discharge, deposit, injection, dumping, spilling, leaking, or placing of any solid waste or hazardous waste into or on any land or water so that such solid waste or hazardous waste or any constituent thereof may enter the environment or be emitted into the air or discharged into any waters, including ground waters".[34] "Disposal" of a hazardous substance includes even a minor neutralization of the substance. Persons who have "arranged" the disposal or treatment of a hazardous substance do not need to know the location where the hazardous substance is disposed of. Such PRPs include "persons whose used oil was collected and transported to an oil recycling facility, and persons who disposed of lead-acid batteries or transformers containing polychlorinated biphenyls (PCBs)

[31] US Environmental Protection Agency, Superfund: National Priorities List (NPL); https://www.epa.gov/superfund/superfund-national-priorities-list-npl.

[32] 42 United States Code paragraph 9601(9).

[33] Ibid paragraph 9601(14).

[34] Ibid paragraph 9601(29); see ibid. s 6903(3).

at a junkyard, and persons who arranged for the disposal of hazardous substances at landfills".[35]

5 Waste as an Environmental Risk

There is no consistent concept of risk in research processes. The scientific approach to risk has undergone continuous evolution over time. Consequently, contemporary scholars tend to utilise a multitude of definitions of risk that are frequently incompatible or incoherent.[36] In the past, there were numerous, albeit ultimately unsuccessful, attempts to address this lack of clarity. Not one of the proposed definitions was accepted by all researchers or practitioners within various fields of social activity. Nevertheless, all of the various definitions refer to categories that emerge in the future and to values that defining subjects share.

In the course of risk studies (generally conducted by economists), two essential trends were identified and established. The first of these approaches views risk as a function of the attributes inherent to its source. In accordance with this trend, risk is regarded as an objective and independent phenomenon, distinct from the beliefs of an individual. It is assessed in terms of expertise, employing measures such as the probability of occurrence or the potential scope of damage. The attitudes of individuals towards an objectively existing risk are shaped by their perception of that risk. The alternative approach regards risk as a phenomenon that is subject-centred, individual and subjective. This approach does not allow external entities to identify the risk, as it is determined by a range of internal factors specific to the subject of risk. Therefore, the characteristics of risk are inherently variable, contingent on the subject to which the risk pertains. This approach allows for the analysis of risk using measurements of the probability of damage realisation, or the potential scope of such damage. It does not, however, preclude the use of probabilistic methods of risk assessment. The values of these measures will remain variable depending on the subject of risk under consideration. The analysis of the subjective factor in risk studies brings together the conclusions of both trends.[37] The demand for insurance protection is either derived from identification of particular individual risk category by the potential insured person (subjective approach to risk) or results from a definite perception of an objectively existing risk (objective approach to risk).

Within the lengthy and abundant history of risk studies, it was only in mid-twentieth century that environmental risk became a subject of researchers' interest. In the twentieth century environmental risk started to be linked to technological

[35] Fogleman (2024), pp. 178–184.

[36] Aven (2010), pp. 95: 623–631. Rejda (2017), Renn (1998), pp. 49–71.; Vaughan and Vaughan (2008).

[37] For an extensive discussion on this topic see Lemkowska (2024), pp. 254–270.

development.[38] Until mid-twentieth century the benefits resulting from exploration of technology were believed to outbalance the costs represented by materialisation of environmental risk. It was only in the 1960s that environmental issues were recognised as socially relevant.[39] Research on this topic was markedly extended at the beginning of the twenty-first century, driven largely by the emergence of more stringent global environmental regulations that established clear standards for environmental liability.[40] In the past 50 years, the scientific approach to environmental risk (just as to risk in general) has significantly evolved. The evolution concerned the entitlements the entities were granted to define the values which are violated by materialisation of environmental risk.[41] Risk originates from all types of relations of the subject at risk with the environment. The subject of environmental risk can be a natural person, a legal person or a legal entity with limited legal capacity, whose property or personal interests may be infringed as a result of their relations with the environment. Not every subject's relationship with the environment will constitute an environmental risk. It only results from the accidental impact on the elements of the environment. It indicates inadvertent and socially unacceptable impact on the environment.

Nuisance can also be considered an environmental risk. There are two types of common-law nuisance: private nuisance and public nuisance. A public nuisance is an unreasonable, unjustified or unlawful interference with a right that is shared by the general public. Unlike a private nuisance, a public nuisance must affect more than one person—sometimes an entire community or neighbourhood, depending on the state. The use of land to dump toxic waste is an example of a public nuisance. There is a case where people living near a clearing in the woods that was used by the defendants to store and dispose of more than 100 deteriorating drums with liquid hazardous waste filed a nuisance lawsuit. Explosions at the site led to a massive fire. The court easily concluded that the defendants had caused a private and public nuisance and issued an injunction to prevent them from accepting further waste and to clean up the existing pollution. Eventually, the site was placed under the Superfund program.

A nuisance can be permanent or continuing. Depending on the state, the differentiating factor may be whether the nuisance can be stopped or abated, as well as (or instead) the period during which it occurs. An example is a case that went before the Maine Supreme Judicial Court. The court ruled that in a case where the plaintiff

---

[38] Stankiewicz (2008), pp. 55–72, idem, Ryzyko i konflikt. Strategie zarządzania konfliktami technologicznymi w Polsce. Dissertation, Uniwersytet Mikołaja Kopernika 2008.

[39] The statement by The Secretary General of the United Nations U'Thant at the 23rd session during the UN Assembly in 1968 followed a year later by a document "Problems of the Human Environment" (called "U'Thant's Report") marked the symbolic beginning of the contemporary approach of the international community to the issue of environmental risk.

[40] Bamberg and Möser (2007), pp. 14–25. Xu et al. (2017), pp. 35–50; Janmaimool and Watanabe (2014), pp. 6291–6313., Altonoğlu et al. (2017), pp. 436–444.; Rowe and Frewer (2004), pp. 512–556.

[41] See more broadly Lemkowska (2024), pp. 269–270.

acquired land contaminated with waste deposited before 1978, there was a question of fact regarding the existence of a permanent or continuing nuisance. The relevant factual issue was whether the contamination could be cleaned up and thus abated. Under Maine law, a continuing nuisance exists if it can be abated. This rule is relevant to the statute of limitations.

If the nuisance could be abated, the plaintiff's action would not be time-barred, because a continuing nuisance results in a new cause of action for each day that the nuisance continues. If the nuisance could not be abated, the plaintiff's action would be time barred under the six-year statute of limitations under Maine law. The remedies for nuisance are compensatory damages for past (and in some cases future) harm and/or a prohibitory injunction. A public nuisance can be both a civil and criminal offence, although the introduction of specific offenses in statutory law in many states abolished the nuisance as a crime.

6 Environmental Damage as a Consequence of a Waste Risk

Pollution (emissions causing specific negative consequences) is materialisation of environmental risk. These negative consequences can affect the property and personal interests of third parties as well as the polluter himself.. Pollution results in damage to the environment. There is no universal, globally applicable legal definition of damage to the environment. Since the twentieth century many notions have been developed to refer to the recently recognized damage, both in legislation and literature. Currently, the terms "environmental damage" or "ecological damage" are most commonly used in the literature. They are usually treated as synonyms, but also as concepts with differing meanings.

Liu Jing opted for the concept of "ecological damage" as one "which comprises not only damage to public natural recourses but also damage to owned resources". Furthermore, according to the author, this concept can fit into traditional tort law. The term "ecological damage" emphasizes that it is about "loss or damage to the environment, rather than personal injury, property damage and economic loss caused via the environment". It encompasses both the damage to components of the environment that are unowned and to owned parts that have an ecological value exceeding the personal value to the owners.[42] This approach to defining "ecological damage" is consistent with some characteristics in the definition of ecological damage identified in the literature: "a detrimental physical change of the environment, that does not – or not only- affect personal property, health or economic interests, but injures the public interest in the conservation and use of the environment".[43]

However, the term "environmental damage" is widely used both at the regional and national level. What is particularly important for research focusing on European

[42] Jing (2013), pp. 17–18, 34–40.

[43] Bocken (1997), pp. 150–152, 157.

solutions under ELD (Environmental Liability Directive), a harmonised liability system is established for "environmental damage.[44] Only biodiversity damage, water damage and land damage are classified as "environmental damage". Biodiversity damage should be defined as the damage to any species or habitat protected under Council Directive 79/409/EEC of 2 April 1979 on the Conservation of Wild Birds,[45] Council Directive 92/43/EEC on the Conservation of Natural Habitats and of Wild Fauna and Flora (the Habitat Directive).[46] Water damages is limited by the categories defined in Directive 2000/60/EC of the European Parliament and of the Council establishing a framework for the Community action in the field of water policy (Water Framework Directive).[47] When it comes to the geographical location, the biodiversity damage and water damage should also be "significantly adverse". As regards the third category: "land damage", the threshold is determined by its risk for human health instead of the adverse changes to the land itself.

In accordance with the broadest terminology developed by the literature, environmental damage encompasses both primary damage (done to the elements of the environment) and secondary damage (done to a person, property or causing financial losses of indirectly affected parties). The particular elements of the environment can also be private property (land), or constitute the common good (air), which determines the type of risk assigned to particular victims.[48] In the broader sense, "environmental damage" refers to the damage caused via the environment, including damage to public natural resources and also damage to the owned parts of the environment, and even consequential losses such as a pure economic loss, cleanup costs and personal injury.[49] According to the literature, "environmental damage" may be understood also in narrower sense, where damage to persons or property is excluded. The term "environmental damage" is then understood as "damage done to the com-

---

[44] According to Article 2.1. "environmental damage" means: "damage to protected species and natural habitats, which is any damage that has significant adverse effects on reaching or maintaining the favourable conservation status of such habitats or species. (…) b) 'water damage', which is any damage that significantly adversely affects: (i) the ecological, chemical or quantitative status or the ecological potential, as defined in Directive 2000/60/EC, of the waters concerned, with the exception of adverse effects where Article 4(7) of that Directive applies; or (ii) the environmental status of the marine waters concerned, as defined in Directive 2008/56/EC, in so far as particular aspects of the environmental status of the marine environment are not already addressed through Directive 2000/60/EC; (c) land damage, which is any land contamination that creates a significant risk of human health being adversely affected as a result of the direct or indirect introduction, in, on or under land, of substances, preparations, organisms or micro-organisms".

[45] Council Directive 79/409/EEC of 2 April 1979 on the conservation of wild birds, OJ L 103, 25.4.1979, pp. 1–18.

[46] Council Directive 92/43/EEC of 21 May 1992 on the conservation of natural habitats and of wild fauna and flora, OJ L 206, 22.7.1992, pp. 7–50.

[47] Directive 2000/60/EC of the European Parliament and of the Council of 23 October 2000 establishing a framework for Community action in the field of water policy, OJ L 327, 22.12.2000, pp. 1–73.

[48] Swiss Re (2007). Insuring environmental damage in the European Union. www.swissre.com. Accessed 15 Jan 2014.

[49] Brans (2001), p. 13.

ponents of the environment, as well as the loss of diminution of environmental values caused by the deterioration or destruction of such components.[50]

The lack of consistency in defining this type of damage is reflected in international regulations. International legal acts (conventions) treat environmental issues in a "spotlight" manner, as environmental damage refers to a particular type of activity there.[51] International regulations serve to address transboundary environmental damage. They establish rules for remedying damage that apply only when several countries are involved.[52] The concept of "pollution damage" is used frequently by international treaties.[53] However, they may include some components which are relevant for damage to the environment. From the research issues point of view, Basel Protocol on Liability and Compensation for Damage Resulting from Transboundary Movements of Hazardous Waste and Their Disposal is noteworthy. The protocol gives no specific name to such damage but it allows the compensation for "costs of measures of reinstatements of the impaired environment" and "the cost of preventive measures".[54]

The indicated international legislation is an expression of the older definitions. Definitions of this generation often focus on damage caused by specific sources. Modern definitions tend to be more general, refer to the whole environment and shif the focus from human use to ecological effects. Therefore, the term "pollution damage", used in the twentieth century, is being replaced by the term "environmental damage" or "ecological damage". An analysis of the history of pollution legislation

[50] Barboza (1977), p. 76.

[51] e.g. Convention on liability and compensation for damage in connection with the carriage of hazardous and noxious substances by sea, 1996, type of emissions (Convention on civil liability for oil pollution damage, 1969; Protocol to amend the international Convention on civil liability for oil pollution damage, 1984) or precisely defined element of the environment (e.g. the seas) (Convention on the Law of the Sea, 1982) Lugano Convention (Convention on civil liability for damage resulting from activities dangerous to the environment, 1993). The document regulated the liability for the broadly meant environmental damage without the limitations regarding the type of activity, emissions, or the element of the environment. The convention, however, never came into force.

[52] Khalatbari and Poorhashemi (2019).

[53] For example, the International Convention on Civil Liability for Oli Pollution Damage 1969 (the CLC 1969) defined "pollution damage" as: "loss or damage caused outside the ship carrying oil by contamination resulting from the escape or discharge of oil from the ship, wherever such escape or discharge may occur, and include the cost of preventive measures and further loss of damage caused preventive measures".

[54] According to Article 2 (2c) of Basel Protocol on Liability and Compensation for Damage Resulting from Transboundary Movements of Hazardous Waste and Their Disposal, Basel 10 December 1999,l UN Doc. UNEP/CHW 1/WG/1/9/2. "Damage" means: (i) Loss of life or personal injury; (ii) Loss of or damage to property other than property held by the person liable in accordance with the present Protocol; (iii) Loss of income directly deriving from an economic interest in any use of the environment, incurred as a result of impairment of the environment, taking into account savings and costs; (iv) The costs of measures of reinstatement of the impaired environment, limited to the costs of measures actually taken or to be undertaken; and (v) The costs of preventive measures, including any loss or damage caused by such measures, to the extent that the damage arises out of or results from hazardous properties of the wastes involved in the transboundary movement and disposal of hazardous wastes and other wastes subject to the Convention.

reveals a shift in the definition of pollution damage: the older definitions focus on activities that affect the utility of a resource for humans, while the second generation shifts the focus to the ecological effects of the resource. Similar to "environmental damage" in a broader sense, the concept of pollution damage includes both damage to the environment and typical damage to individuals(personal injury and property damage).[55]

Waste as a source of pollution may result in environmental damage. Compensation of such damages faces some obstacles from traditional tort law. In traditional tort law, the relationship between legally protected rights and interests and actual loss determines whether a loss is qualified as a damage.[56] Both property and non-property damage require an individual violation of rights or interests, which is the main difficulty in considering damage to non-owned natural resources as compensable damage. Some damages are irreversible: the cost of the resource affects its availability. In such a case, the damage is also not compensable. Furthermore, the difficulty of identifying affected parties also prevents compensation for damage to public natural resources. Public natural resources, depending on the legal system, are understood as not owned by anyone (in the U.S.) or being in the public domain (in Europe). In the first case, the claim cannot be based on ownership, which is usually the case for property damage. In the U.S., public authorities are given standing on the basis of trusteeship and *parens patriae.* In the European legal system, collective harm are rarely considered compensable. The authorization is based on the duties of government or other interest rather than property rights, which requires the legal development outside of the domain of traditional tort law.

One of the features which prevents full compensation through traditional tort law is that the primary remedy for environmental damage is restoration and not monetary compensation.[57] The emphasis on restoration leads to more government intervention (the executive authority). When there is imminent threat of environmental damage if damage occurs, further damage should be prevented by appropriate measures, and it is not sufficient to simply to clean up and restore the area. Restoration is a method of transforming damage to un-owned natural resource into a monetary loss suffered by the person who took the restorative measures. Restoration helps to individualize the collective interests that have been infringed and thus the damage can be classified as a pecuniary damage.[58]

An example of restoration of environmental damage is soil remediation due to a damage caused by waste management, if the remediation is carried out by a specialised entity on the basis of a administrative authority's decision. The cost of such restoration is covered by the polluting waste holder (or his insurer).

The entities liable for the management of waste are typically the first to become aware of the existence or threat of damage. Consequently, they are in a position to

[55] Larsson (1999), pp. 158, 172, 175.

[56] See L. Jing, Compensating Ecological Damage. Comparative and Economic Observations ... p. 42.

[57] See L. Jing, Compensating Ecological Damage ..., p. 38.

[58] See L. Jing, Compensating Ecological ..., pp. 36, 42.

take prompt preventive and clean-up action. However, the entities liable for management of waste may lack the requisite expertise to remediate natural resources effectively and may attempt to externalise costs by undertaking insufficient restorative actions. In contrast, public environmental authorities may possess more information and expertise regarding certain natural resources and their appropriate restoration. Consequently, it is common practice for public authorities to intervene in the environmental restoration process.[59] A mix of public and civil elements "may influence the operation of compensation instruments and requires cooperation between public authorities and the providers of compensation instruments".[60] The proof of causation and identification of injuries still prove to be obstacles for compensation. The level of probability of causation in traditional tort law is usually quite high for the cases of environmental damage. Even if the causal link between one kind of activity and the damage is established, the involvement of multiple actors still results in a challenge to identify whose activity and to what extent is responsible for a specific damage. Some special arrangements needs to be made for environmental damage, such as the links between administrative requirements s and assessment rules. Insurance, as a compensation mechanism, may cover such specific damage (discussed in more detail in chapter "Waste Insurance Guarantee").

The occurrence of environmental damage may be attributed to a number of different activities, including both those that result in industrial pollution and activities that are not associated with pollution. In accordance with the ELD regime, both contamination and non-contamination incidents may result in a response action and the assumption of liability. The ELD defines damage to protected species, natural habitats and water damage in accordance with the extent and scope of the damage to these resources. The ELD identifies certain activities (listed in Annex III) as potential triggers of environmental damage. Waste management is also recognized as such factors, as evidenced in section 2: "Waste management operations, including the collection, transport, recovery and disposal of waste and hazardous waste, including the supervision of such operations and after-care of disposal sites, subject to permit or registration in pursuance of Council Directive 75/442/EEC of 15 July 1975 on waste (2) and Council Directive 91/689/EEC of 12 December 1991 on hazardous waste (3). Those operations include, inter alia, the operation of landfill sites under Council Directive 1999/31/EC of 26 April 1999 on the landfill of waste (4) and the operation of incineration plants under Directive 2000/76/EC of the European Parliament and of the Council of 4 December 2000 on the incineration of waste" and section 12, concerning transboundary shipment of waste. These activities include both polluting and non-polluting incidents, which is important for waste assessment as an environmental risk. It is noteworthy that the majority of existing compensation mechanisms were designed to address pollution incidents, while non-polluting incidents remain largely unregulated. This discrepancy can be attributed to several factors, including the limited experience of insurers in providing

59 Boyd (2003), pp. 266–267.

60 L. Jing, Compensating ecological …, p. 38.

environmental insurance products and the lack of public awareness regarding the ELD's coverage of non-polluting incidents.[61]

References

Altonoğlu BD, Atav E, Sönmez S (2017) The investigation of environmental risk perception and attitudes towards the environment in secondary school students. Turkish Online J Edu Technol 436–444

Aven T (2010) On how to define, understand and describe risk. Reliability Engineering and System Safety

Bamberg S, Möser G (2007) Twenty years after Hines, Hungerford, and Tomera: a new meta-analysis of psycho-social determinants of pro-environmental behavior. J Environ Psychol 27:14–25

Barboza J (1977) The ILC and environmental damage. In: Wetterstein P (ed) Harm to the environment: the right to compensation and the assessment of damage. Clarendon Press, Oxford

Bocken H (1997) The compensation of ecological damage in Belgium. In: Wtterstein P (ed) Harm to the environment: the right in compensation and the assessment of damages. Clarendon Press, Oxford, pp 150–152

Boyd J (2003) A market-based analysis of financial insurance issues associated with US natural resources damage liability. In: Faure M (ed) Deterrence, insurability with compensation in environment liability. Future development in the European Union, Vienna. Springer, New York

Brans EHP (2001) Liability for damages to public natural resources. Kluwer Law International, The Hague

Fogleman V (2024) Environmental liabilities and insurance law in the United States. In: Maśniak D, Malinowska K (eds) Managing environmental risk through insurance. Springer

Janmaimool P, Watanabe T (2014) Evaluating determinants of environmental risk perception for risk management in contaminated sites. Int J Environ Res Public Health 11(6):6291–6313

Jing L (2013) Compensation ecological damage. Comparative and economic observation, Cambridge

Khalatbari Y, Poorhashemi A (2019) "Environmental damage": challenges and opportunities in international environmental law. CIFILE J Int Law 1(1)

Larsson ML (1999) Legal definitions of the environment and of the environmental damage. In: Wahlgren P (ed) Scandinavian studies in law, Volume 38. Legal Issues of the Law 1990s. Stockholm Institute for Scandinavian Law, Stockholm

Lemkowska M (2024) Environmental insurance product. In: Malinowska K, Maśniak D (eds) Managing environmental risks through insurance. Springer

Rejda G (2017) Principles of risk management and insurance, Global Edition. Pearson Education Limited

Renn O (1998) Three decades of risk research: accomplishments and new challenges. J Risk Res 1:49–71

Rowe GR, Frewer LJ (2004) Evaluating public participation exercises: a research agenda. Science Technol Human Values October

[61] Report from the Commission to the Council, the European Parliament, the European Economic and Social Committee and the Committee of Tte Regions under Article 14(2) of Directive 2004/35/CE on the environmental liability with regard to the prevention and remedying of environmental damage, Brussels, 12.10.2010 COM(2010) 581 final.

Smith A (2001) Keith Brown, Steve Ogilvie, Kathryn Rushton, Judith Bates, waste management options and climate change. Final report to the European Commission, DG Environment, July 2001

Stankiewicz P (2008) Invisible risk. The social construction of security. Polish Sociol Rev 1(161):55–72

Vaughan EJ, Vaughan T (2008) Fundamentals of risk and insurance, 11th edn. John Wiley and Sons Inc

Xu G, Feng X, Li Y, Chen X, Jia J (2017) Environmental risk perception and its influence on well-being. Chinese Manage Stud 11(1):35–50

Principles Supporting the Development of the Waste Insurance

1 Introduction

This chapter identifies the legal principles that provide the conceptual foundation for integrating insurance mechanisms into waste management. The selection focuses on four principles rooted in EU law, reflecting the European orientation of the research, while acknowledging that the relevance of the prevention and precautionary principles extends beyond the EU legal order. Both principles play a central role in environmental law and offer important support for strengthening the preventive dimension of waste insurance. Their emphasis on anticipating and mitigating environmental harm aligns with the broader shift within risk governance from compensatory approaches toward preventive strategies. For this reason, the chapter outlines their conceptual framework. and clarifies their significance for insurance-based instruments.

Another principle essential for developing waste insurance is the polluter pays principle, which—when applied to waste management—takes the more operationally accurate form of the waste holder pays principle. This formulation positions the waste holder as the entity responsible for the environmental consequences arising from waste handling. Related to this is the principle of extended producer responsibility (EPR), which assigns responsibilities throughout the entire life cycle of a product, including the stage in which it becomes waste. Unlike the polluter pays principle, which focuses on the harmful effects of specific activities, EPR links producers to the financial and organisational duties associated with the management of products after their use.

Finally, the analysis situates these principles within broader policy frameworks. The life-cycle approach embedded in EPR closely corresponds to the logic of the circular economy model, which promotes resource efficiency, recovery, and reuse. Additionally, the evolving concept of Environmental, Social and Governance (ESG) criteria provides a wider normative context for defining responsibility for

D. Maśniak, *The Legal Framework for the Use of Insurance in Ecological Waste Management*, AIDA Europe Research Series on Insurance Law and Regulation 17, https://doi.org/10.1007/978-3-032-26550-0_3

environmental impacts, including those generated by waste management. Together, these principles and policy frameworks establish a coherent basis for understanding how insurance can support environmentally sound and legally robust waste-management systems.

2 Prevention Principle and Precautionary Principle

2.1 *Prevention Principle and Precautionary Principle in International and EU Environmental Law*

The preventive principle and the precautionary principle are the guiding principles of international environmental law. The international law doctrine indicates that these two principles can be clearly distinguished from each other: prevention concerns tangible risks, whereas precaution concerns scientific uncertainty. Risks fall under the principle of prevention if the causal link between an event and damage is established by irrefutable scientific evidence,. Such risks can be described as certain, because it is possible to establish the causal link between the initial event and its adverse effects, and to calculate the probability of their occurrence. Precaution represents a paradigm shift as it is characterized by uncertainty. In fact, precaution does not presuppose perfect understanding of a given risk. It is enough that risk is suspected, assumed or feared of. In such a situation, the thresholds at which precautionary action should be taken in order to avoid or minimise the occurrence of the risk cannot be determined. In other words, precaution means that the absence of scientific certainty as to the existence or extent of a risk should no longer delay the adoption of preventive measures to protect the environment. To sum up, the precautionary approach requires the decisionmaker to intervene, provided that two conditions are met: the threats to the environment are tangible, and the authorities, in accordance with the precautionary principle, are prepared to address risks for which there is no definitive proof either that there is a causal link between the predicted activity and the damage, or that the predicted damage will materialise.[1] The precautionary principle has been the subject of controversy, and its critics have been confused as to the scope and the status of the principle. As a matter of fact, disputes have arisen as to whether precaution[2] should be labelled as a "principle" or merely as an "approach", what would distinguish a legal principle from a political approach.

In real life, the distinction between preventing and taking precautions is not always so clear-cut. There is, in a sense, a continuum that runs from the certainty that underlies preventive action to the precautionary action that is triggered by uncertainty. Preventive measures may become precautionary when they become entangled in scientific uncertainty. On the other hand, if scientists are able to resolve

[1] De Sadeleer (2010), p. 168.

[2] Peel (2005), pp. 483–501.

remaining uncertainties, the nature of initially precautionary measures can become more preventive.

The prevention principle has been incorporated into many international instruments. Thus, Rio's Principle 2 entails a paradigm shift in placing greater emphasis on preventing damage in general rather than on the damage caused to the sovereign rights of other states. The reference to "areas beyond the limits of national jurisdiction" laid the groundwork for a more comprehensive notion of prevention that is no longer restricted solely to bilateral relations.[3] The principles contained in the 1992 Rio de Janeiro Declaration[4] are widely recognised by states and provide practical guidance on development and the application of international law. According to Rio Principle 5, "in order to protect the environment, the precautionary approach shall be widely applied by States according to their capabilities".[5] In The Treaty on European Union (Maastricht Treaty), it is stated that "the Community that preventative action should be taken, that environmental damage should as a priority be rectified at source and that the polluter should pay. Environmental protection requirements must be integrated into the definition and implementation of other Community policies".[6] Prevention is now widely recognised as a rule of customary international law, placing preventive duties on the states to carry out activities within their territory or under their jurisdiction.

Prevention is a core function of environmental law. Preventive measures aim to avoid materialisation of environmental damage risk. The impossibility of restoring the environment to its state before pollution determines the importance of this function. This has also been noted by the International Court of Justice (ICJ). In particular, the Gabčíkovo–Nagymaros case reflects the importance afforded by the ICJ to prevention: "in the field of environmental protection, vigilance and prevention are required on account of the often irreversible character of damage to the environment and of the limitations inherent in the very mechanism of reparation of this type of damage[7]". According to the ICJ, the principle of prevention, as customary law, has its origins in the due diligence incumbent upon each state within its own territory.[8]

Prevention principle is reflected in regional law, and EU law is its best example. The prevention principle as well as precautionary principle have been proclaimed in Article 191 (2) of the Treaty on the Functioning of the European Union (TFEU), which states that "Union policy on the environment (…) shall be based on the precautionary principle and on the principles that preventive action should be taken". It also strengthens one of the objectives assigned to EU environment policy

[3] Duvic-Paoli (2018), p. 9.

[4] Rio Declaration on Environment and Development included in the report of the United Nations Conference on Environment and Development (Rio De Janeiro, 3–14 June 1992).

[5] IISD 2020 International Institute for Sustainable Development, The precautionary principle, October 2020.

[6] Treat on European Union (Maastricht Treaty), Consolidated version 2016, OJ C 202, 7.6.2016, Article 130r.

[7] Case Concerning the Gabčíkovo–Nagymaros Project (Hungary v. Slovakia) (1997), ICJ Rep. 7.

[8] Duvic-Paoli (2018), pp. 91–135.

in Article 191(1): namely, "to ensure a prudent and rational utilisation of natural resources". Treaty-based secondary law clarifies the obligations arising from the prevention principle. An example of this is the Environmental Liability Directive—so-called Environmental Directive 2004/35/WE[9]), which imposes an obligation on entities undertaking activities that may have a negative impact on the environment to prevent such an impact, and on entities undertaking activities whose negative impact on the environment is not yet entirely recognised, to take all possible preventive measures in a precautionary manner. As a consequence of these obligations, potential polluters are obliged to bear the costs of preventing such pollution.

However, according to the Directive, preventive measures cover not only the responsibility of private actors, but are also addressed to public authorities, as they are responsible for ensuring that the liable actors themselves take or finance the necessary preventive or remedial measures.[10] Numerous preventive mechanisms in EU secondary law—environmental impact assessments, notification procedures, adequate control of risks, exchange of data on the effects of harmful activities, etc. play a crucial role in preventing environmental damage and thus give substance to the principle. Importantly, in waste management, prevention takes precedence over other operations such as reuse, recycling, recovery and disposal (Article 4 of the Waste Directive). Thus, the CJEU has ruled that "the principles of precaution and preventive action oblige the [EU] and the Member States to anticipate, reduce and, as far as possible, to cut off at their origin sources of pollution or nuisances through the adoption of measures intended to eliminate known risks (…) To the extent that wastes, even those in temporary storage, may give rise to serious damage to the environment, there is reason to consider that the provisions of [the Waste FD] which aims to implement the precautionary principle, are equally applicable to operations involving temporary storage".[11]

The analysis of recent treaty and case law developments signals a shift from the traditional negative aspects of prevention (ensuring that activities within their jurisdiction or control do not cause damage to the environment of other states or of areas beyond the limits of national jurisdiction) towards a duty to take all appropriate measures with a view to preventing significant harm to the environment. What is important, the analysis also highlights the pivotal role of different substantive and procedural duties in framing the content of the due diligence. Under EU law, the principle of prevention is fairly complex, owing to the number and diversity of the legal instruments in which it occurs.[12]

[9] Directive 2004/35/CE of the European Parliament and of the Council of 21 April 2004 on environmental liability with regard to the prevention and remedying of environmental damage *OJ L 143, 30.4.2004, p. 56–75.*

[10] Noussia (2023) pp. 100–111.

[11] C-175/98 and C-177/98, Francesca Bizzaro et Paolo Lirussi, 1999: paras 51–3.

[12] de Sadeleer (2010), p. 167.

Unlike the prevention principle, the precautionary principle failed to secure a strong position in waste management law. The 1991 Bamako Convention[13] on the Ban of the Import into Africa and the Control of Transboundary Movement and Management of Hazardous Wastes within Africa defines the precautionary approach as including, inter alia, "preventing the release into the environment of substances which may cause harm to humans or the environment without waiting for scientific proof regarding such harm" (Article 4(3)(f)). The precautionary principle is one of the pillars of the EU environmental policy. As set out in paragraph 2 of Article 192 of the TFEU: "Union policy on the environment ... shall be based on the precautionary principle". As a result, institutions as well as Member States are obliged to apply the principle while carrying out action in the environment.[14] The precautionary principle has been fleshed out in a broad range of measures, starting from notification procedures, prior authorisation schemes, restrictions on the use or the sale of a product, and safeguard clauses,[15] to bans.[16] The regulatory approach is not always consistent. Some EU legislation refers to the principle whereas other legislation on similar topics may ignore it (as in waste management).

2.2 *Insurance Prevention Principle*

In property insurance, the compensatory function is considered predominant. Methodologically, however, the preventive function has also always been perceptible.[17] This change can be seen in new innovative insurance products.

Prevention can make the insurance claims process more sustainable.[18] The preventive function of environmental insurance is related to its social impact and the possibility of supporting state action in this regard. The compensatory function of insurance is beneficial for the insured, but it creates moral hazard. It is through the compulsory preventive action imposed on the policyholder that this temptation is reduced. Prevention is the most rational method of loss control. A paradigm shift from risk transfer to risk prevention is currently tangible.

Both practitioners and legal academics as well as commentators specializing in insurance law draw attention to the role of insurers in supporting risk mitigation by

---

[13] Bamako Convention on the Ban of the Import into Africa and the Control of Transboundary Movement and Management of Hazardous Wastes within Africa, Bamako 30.01.1991.

[14] Judgment of the Court (Grand Chamber) of 7 September 2004. Landelijke Vereniging tot Behoud van de Waddenzee and Nederlandse Vereniging tot Bescherming van Vogels v Staatssecretaris van Landbouw, Natuurbeheer en Visserij.Case C-127/02.

[15] Judgment of the Court of 21 March 2000. Association Greenpeace France and Others v Ministère de l'Agriculture et de la Pêche and Others.Case C-6/99.

[16] Judgment of the Court of First Instance (Third Chamber) of 11 September 2002. Pfizer Animal Health SA v Council of the European Union. Case T-13/99. para. 457.

[17] Sangowski (2001), pp. 102–103.

[18] Ibidem, pp. 100–101.

policyholders by improving the effectiveness of communication tools through the use of technological advances, such as the Internet or smartphones. Today, insurers encourage policyholders to use network connected devices such as water leak detectors or smart smoke detectors.

Nothing prevents them from being waste management risk prevention tools used at both risk estimation and insurance premium determination stages. An example of such tools may be risk monitoring systems with sensors that can detect contamination and improve remote and continuous monitoring of soil, air and groundwater.[19] The new business model involves insurance risk mitigation services provided by the insurers[20] through appropriate devices connected to the network, which modifies the perception of the insurance business. As highlighted in the UN report, insurance has the power to "support businesses in their endeavours while better understanding, preventing and reducing pollution risks and other environmentally-damaging events",[21] fitting into the culture of prevention. Technological development not only influences the identification of factors that increase the risk of environmental damage. It also increases the ability to react quickly when there is an opportunity to limit the extent of such damage. Prevention in waste insurance refers to underwriting, when the policyholder (here: the waste holder demonstrating how the site is secured or the technologies adopted in the operation) behaviour risk is identified. It also concerns the execution of an insurance contract, when it involves stimulating the policyholder behaviour by encouraging or imposing good waste management practices aimed at mitigating the effects of damaging events. Technological solutions also make it possible to predict the outcome of insureds behaviour and even track the behaviour of insureds by relying on devices connected to the network. Such possibilities become particularly crucial in cases of landfill insurance where a decision by an environmental authority is a prerequisite for compensation payment. Data from new sources, processed better and in greater quantity, can potentially facilitate the implementation of advanced risk management and early warning systems.

The systems, in turn, enable timely interventions to not only reduce the frequency of insured events, but also reduce the severity of the damage when the risk materialises. The importance of data for risk prevention purposes is confirmed by the research presented in the UN report. It shows the need for insurers to obtain data on preventive measures taken to mitigate the effects of pollution, which will enable them to increase the potential of environmental insurance.[22] In environmental insurance, monitoring of the policyholder's activities becomes particularly meaningful.

---

[19] New risks, new opportunities: Harnessing environmental pollution liability insurance for a sustainable economy A global study by UN Environment Programme's Principles for Sustainable Insurance Initiative. United Nations, June 2022 https://www.unepfi.org/wordpress/wp-content/uploads/2022/06/PSI-Life-Health-ESG-Guide.pdf.

[20] Malinowska (2024), pp. 283–299.

[21] Ibidem.

[22] New risks, new opportunities: Harnessing environmental pollution liability insurance for a sustainable economy A global study by UN Environment Programme's Principles for Sustainable Insurance Initiative. Unites Nations,. June 2022.

Therefore, the extent of the obligatory insurance protection is an important issue. When an insurer has access to technological solutions to support prevention, the question arises as to his responsibility to use the technological possibilities not only for own profits, but to minimise the insurance risk also in the interest of the insured and, in the case of waste insurance, more broadly in the interest of society. Hence, there is a strong connection between the principle of insurance prevention and the classic principles of insurance law—the principle of utmost good faith and the principle of indemnity[23] in the spirit of the ESG concept (discussed below). The insurer has access not only to data the customer can be asked for, but also the data possible to obtain from many different sources, without the involvement or even knowledge of the potential insured. This new reality has been recognised by regulators and taken into account in the Artificial Intelligence Act.[24]

It is also at the heart of proposing the concept of open insurance. The concept of open insurance is part of the concept of open finance based on the broader idea of access to data. In its previous work, EIOPA has considered open insurance in the broadest sense, encompassing access to and sharing of personal and non-personal insurance-related data, typically through application programming interfaces (APIs). EIOPA attempted to look at them from a client, supervisory and industry perspective. Preliminary analysis indicates that the exchange of data (both personal and non-personal) via (open) APIs has emerged in the insurance sector and can facilitate industry-wide innovation and increase the flexibility of companies to respond to changes in customer needs and expectations.[25] Due to its universality and social role, EIOPA's research has so far concerned motor insurance. However, there is no doubt that the theses formulated by the experts concerning the role of access to data collected by insurers also apply to other insurances, in particular insurances of social importance, which include waste insurance.

By causing firms to internalise potential damages, these policies have the potential to change in the market and the amount of precaution that companies take. Financial security (that may take the form of waste insurance) achieves the preventive function of environmental liability, while overcoming the shortcomings of limited liability (characteristic for companies).[26] The preventive function of environmental liability requires the waste holder to repair the environmental damage caused by their activities.[27] If a rational waste holder was held financially liable, he would seek to increase his level of care in order to reduce the level of environmental

---

[23] See more broadly Malinowska (2024), pp. 283–300.

[24] Regulation (EU) 2024/1689 of the European Parliament and the Council of 13 June 2024 laying down harmonised rules on artificial intelligence and amending Regulations (EC) No 300/2008, (EU) No 167/2013, (EU) No 168/2013, (EU) 2018/858, (EU) 2018/1139 and (EU) 2019/2144 and Directives 2014/90/EU, (EU) 2016/797 and (EU) 2020/1828 (Artificial Intelligence Act).

[25] Open Insurance: Accessing and sharing insurance-related data, Discussion Paper https://www.eiopa.europa.eu/system/files/2021-01/open-insurance-discussion-paper-28-01-2021.pdf.

[26] The relationship between principle limited liability and financial security is developed in this chapter.

[27] Landini (2013), p. 229.

costs. Failure to take precautionary measures would jeopardise the waste holder's assets.[28] However, this rationale works only if the waste holder has sufficient assets to pay for his environmental costs. If the waste holder's assets are lower than their expected environmental costs, environmental decision-making should give way to profit-maximising decision-making for the benefit of shareholders and, after bankruptcy, creditors.[29] The guarantee instrument (or other financial security instruments) discourages this kind of environmentally irresponsible behaviour by preserving the preventive function—requiring the financial guarantee ex ante—before the environmental damage occurs. If the cost of the guarantee or other financial security (e.g. an insurance contract) corresponds exactly to the expected level of remediation costs, the economic incentive provided by the environmental liability remains effective. The incentive is effective even if the waste holder's assets are insufficient to cover all expected environmental liabilities. This is because all decisions that increase environmental costs are effectively internalised through premiums or other charges. For example, waste holders making environmentally irresponsible decisions on preventive measures are likely to pay higher charges for their guarantee which then is reflected on the price of the product or service they provide.[30]The distinction between preventive and precautionary measures adopted in international law is difficult to apply to insurance law. "Precautionary actions" related to the policyholder are regarded as a way of implementing the preventive function. Despite certain differences between national legal systems, the nature of these obligations is consistent and can be illustrated by the principle included in the PEICL (Principles of European Insurance Contract Law). Article 4:101 of PEICL states that "*A precautionary measure means a clause in the insurance contract, whether or not described as a condition precedent to the liability of the insurer, requiring the policyholder or the insured, before the insured event occurs, to perform or not to perform certain acts. A 'precautionary measures' clause that allows an insurer to refuse to pay all or some of a claim for non-compliance with it, is only effective to the extent the loss was caused by the policyholder or the insured*". A comparative legal analysis of the regulations concerning the policyholder's duty to take precautionary action leads to the conclusion that the burden of most precautionary measures falls on the policyholder who should take reasonable precautions, taking all reasonable steps to safeguard the object of insurance and should aim at minimising the loss by reducing the financial implications of a loss.[31]

Another aspect is the impact of insurance (or other financial security) on the waste holder bankruptcy risk. If they have insurance cover, they are subject to continuous monitoring and risk-based underwriting by the insurer. The risk of bankruptcy also poses a social threat, as the bankruptcy of an entrepreneur affects not only the entrepreneur and his creditors, but also the local economy and, in the case

[28] Colin (2014), pp. 198, 201.

[29] Colin (2014), pp. 192–193.

[30] Colin (2014), pp. 197–198.

[31] See more broadly Basedow et al. (2016), pp. 188–189 and 261.

of large entrepreneurs, the regional economy and society. This is yet another area in which the private and public domains intersect.

The research on the impact of financial security on the risk of business failure in the United States is an example. Major US fossil fuel producing states, US federal land managers, Canadian provinces and other jurisdictions require this type of 'financial assurance' from oil and gas drilling companies. Such requirements are also common in other industries where the credibility of the courts is an issue, including metal mining, landfills, hazardous waste disposal and chemical production.[32] The research showed that there were significant changes in the structure of the industry as a result of the financial security requirement. About 5% of producers left the market immediately. The exiting companies were small and had poor environmental records. Among the remaining companies, the financial assurance requirement reduced the output of 80% of the smallest companies by about 5% on average. The financial assurance requirement moved about 4% of the wells operated by 80% of the smallest companies to new operators. Another 1% of wells operated by these companies was closed, mainly in case of low-producing wells where social costs (including environmental risk) are likely to exceed social benefits. There was also a significant improvement in environmental outcomes. Small producers caused a large share of environmental incidents across the industry, although they accounted for a small part of total production. This meant that the financial assurance requirement had a large impact on the overall environmental costs of oil and gas production, which is expressed by a 70% reduction of around of orphan wells, i.e. wells abandoned by insolvent owners without the necessary precautions to prevent pollution.[33]

3 The Waste Holder Pays Principle as a Modification of the Polluter Pays Principle

The polluter pays principle is a guiding principle at European and international levels.[34] The polluter pays principle is a guiding principle at European and international levels [1]. In accordance with EU legislation, the prevention and compensation for environmental damage should be achieved by promoting the "polluter pays" principle (Article 191 TFEU). This principle is also clearly stated in the Environmental Directive, which stipulates that an entrepreneur who causes damage to the environment through their activities or who poses a direct threat of such damage remains financially responsible for it. The objective of this initiative is to motivate entrepreneurs to adopt measures and cultivate practices that mitigate the risk of environmental degradation, thereby reducing the likelihood of financial liability

32 Boomhower (2019), p. 394.

33 Boomhower (2019), pp. 393, 412–413.

34 Bugge (2009), pp. 411–428.

arising from such damage. Consequently, an entrepreneur who causes damage to the environment through their activities or poses a direct threat of such damage is obliged to bear the costs of the necessary preventive and remedial measures. In light of the distinct nature of environmental degradation, which is a collective good, public entities charged with environmental stewardship are duty-bound to implement preventative and remedial measures autonomously, without awaiting a response from the responsible entrepreneur. In situations where third parties undertake activities on behalf of the entrepreneur, the cost of the measures taken should ultimately be borne by the entrepreneur. It is imperative that these costs encompass the expenses associated with evaluating environmental degradation.[35]

In the context of the polluter pays principle in waste management, Recital 26 of the Waste Directive is noteworthy, according to which: "The waste producer and the waste holder should manage waste in a way that guarantees a high level of protection of the environment and human health"(recital No. 26 of the Waste Directive). In line with this principle, waste disposal costs should be borne by the waste holder or by the previous holders or producers (Article 14 of the Waste Directive). The importance of this principle is also indicated by the EU legislator in the Landfill Directive in the context of waste landfilling, where it is deemed necessary to "take into account any damage to the environment produced by a landfill" (recital No. 5).

In accordance with EU law, the term "waste holder" covers the scope of the waste producer. In accordance with Article 3 point 6 of the Waste Directive, "waste holder means the waste producer or the natural or legal person who is in possession of the waste". However, "waste producer means anyone whose activities produce waste (original waste producer) or anyone who carries out pre-processing, mixing or other operations resulting in a change in the nature or composition of this waste"; (Article 3 (5) of the Waste Directive). The status of waste producer is therefore a factual state and results from the conducted activity or the fact that waste was generated. The status of waste producer can also be obtained as a result of providing services of demolition, renovation of facilities, cleaning of tanks or devices, as well as maintenance and repair.[36]

The waste holder is therefore a broader concept than the generator and involves both the generation of waste and the fact of possession. The use of the term "holder", rather than "owner", indicates the intention of the EU legislator to broadly define the personal scope of application of the polluter pays principle (the reference is to the holder of waste). A holder is a person who has owner-like possession of waste, as well as a person who actually has possession of waste as a user, pledgee, lessee, tenant or having any other right, which entails specific authority over waste owned by another person.

Possession is determined by the factual element in the form of the holder's relationship to the waste—regardless of the legal basis for that possession. The holder's relationship to the waste must be actual, i.e., gives the holder the ability to affect the

[35] Maśniak (2021), p. 95.

[36] Dmowska (2019), p. 135.

waste. Polish legal doctrine emphasizes that the holder cannot be required to maintain physical contact with the object at all times; it is sufficient that he has such a possibility.[37] The possibility of considering a certain factual authority as possession does not depend on the holder's direct control over the objects. In light of this reasoning (common in the civil legislation of many member states), the waste does not lose its status of holder (self-ownership) if the waste is put to use by means of a lease or rental. In addition to actual authority (*corpus*), possession has a second element, i.e. it's exercised by a specific entity in its own interest (*animus rem sibi habendi*).[38]

The holder takes control of the waste at the moment of its actual acquisition, and if he acts in his own interest, he does not lose this possession by giving the waste over to another entity for transportation. That is, at this point he assumes responsibility for waste management and bears the costs of waste disposal and other costs of repairing the environmental damage caused by the waste. The permanence of authority over waste in the self-interest of those deciding to acquire waste holder status is evidenced by an administrative decision. Due to the licensing of waste management, the role of the administrative authority affects the inherently civil law relationship of possession. It is also important from an insurance point of view, since the requirement for financial security (as discussed in more detail below) often arises already at this stage.. In this context, the EU's legislation on cross-border waste transport in Europe deserves attention.

EU law on the shipment of waste includes rules for transporting waste across borders. What draws attention is the far-reaching convergence of the subcategories of the concept of notifier understood as.: "who intends to carry out a shipment of waste or intends to have a shipment of waste carried out and to whom the duty to notify is assigned" (Article 3 point 6 of Regulation on shipments of waste) with the definition of waste holder w Waste Directive. Apart from "authorised dealer or broker" (Article 3point 6 a) IV) the listed subcategories of the concept of notifier (producer, collector—Article 3 point 6 I0, II), III)) can be qualified as a waste holder within the meaning of the Waste Directive[39]). This convergence is also pointed out by the legislator by explicitly referring to the waste holder as a notifer, where all of the specified persons if applicable, „are unknown or insolvent" (Article 3 point 6 (v)). Where the notifier intends to ship he/she shall submit a prior written notification to and through the competent authority of dispatch and a general notification, if it is submitted.. Notification shall be effected by establishing a financial guarantee or an equivalent insurance (Article 5 point 8 of Regulation of Shipments of Waste) – discussed in more detail in the monography. Generally, "the financial guarantee or equivalent insurance (or if the competent authority so allows, evidence of that

[37] Gniewek and Machnikowski (2017).

[38] Cf. E. Skowrońska-Bocian and Warciński (2020), art. 336, nb. 2

[39] Regulation (EU) 2024/1157 of the European Parliament and the Council of April 2024 on shipments of waste, amending Regulation (EU) No 1257/2013 and (EU) 2020/1056 and repealing Regulation (EC) No 1013/2006 *OJ L, 2024/1157, 30.4.2024, EL hereinafter called Regulation on Shipments of Waste.*

guarantee or insurance or a declaration certifying its existence) shall be supplied as part of the notification document at the time of notification".

However, one must agree with the view that under EU waste law, holder is also understood as an illegal holder who does not have permission for waste management in the form of an administrative-legal decision and is not exempt from the obligation to apply for such permission.[40] Excluding such a holder from the PPP would contradict the objectives of the rule.

The waste transporter is also a waste holder, especially when the transport of waste is carried out without the required documents, which indicate the waste holder transferring the waste and the waste holder to whom the waste is to be delivered.[41] Recognizing the transporter as the holder raises doubts due to the difficulty of proving the permanence of the control in the transport.[42] The waste holder is also the surface holder with regard to the waste on the property. Sorting out the subjective scope of the entities responsible for waste management is not facilitated by another important directive on the management of waste from extractive industries,[43] which uses the term "operator" to describe polluter, as stated in recital 25.

In line with recital 34 "The objective of this Directive, that is to say, improving the management of waste from the extractive industries, cannot be sufficiently achieved by the Member States acting alone because the mismanagement of such waste may cause pollution of a transboundary nature. Under the polluter pays principle it is necessary, inter alia, to take into account any damage to the environment caused by waste from the extractive industries, and different national applications of that principle may lead to substantial disparities in the financial burden on economic operators. Moreover, the existence of different national policies on the management of waste from the extractive industries hampers the aim of ensuring a minimum level of safe and responsible management of such waste and maximising its recovery throughout the Community".

The concept of operator has been referred to national regulations on responsibility for managing extractive waste. According to the definition adopted in this directive, it is "the natural or legal person responsible for the management of extractive waste, in accordance with the national law of the Member State in which waste management takes place, including in respect of temporary storage of extractive waste as well as the operational and the after-closure phases" (Article 2. 24). Recognising the concept of waste holder adopted in waste management legislation (Article 2 25) the legislator seems to recognize the need to consider both concepts.

---

[40] See Górski (2005), p. 46.

[41] It is expressly provided by the Act of 20 July 2018 amending the Act on Voivodship Inspectorate of Environmental Protection and other certain acts (Polish Journal of Laws from, item 1479) – Article 24 section 4 a.

[42] Widely. J. Dmowska (2019), p. 137.

[43] Directive 2006/21/EC of the European Parliament and of the Council of 15 March 2006 on the management of waste from extractive industries and amending Directive 2004/35/EC - Statement by the European Parliament, the Council and the Commission *OJ L 102, 11.4.2006, p. 15–34 hereinafter called Extractive Waste Directive.*

This is demonstrated by the operator's responsibility for closure and after-closure procedures for waste facilities. According to Article 12. 1, "The operator shall be responsible for the maintenance, monitoring, control and corrective measures in the after-closure phase for as long as may be required by the competent authority, taking into account the nature and duration of the hazard,(...) without prejudice to any national or Community legislation governing the liability of the waste holder".

The analyse demonstrates that while the polluter pays principle is firmly embedded in EU environmental law, its traditional focus on identifying the actor who "causes" environmental harm is insufficient for the complex realities of waste management. EU waste legislation shows that responsibility does not rest solely with the original waste producer but extends to a broader category of actors—including anyone who possesses, controls, transports, or manages waste, whether legally or illegally. Because "waste holder" is defined broadly to include both factual possession and the ability to influence waste, it captures the full range of entities whose actions determine how waste is handled and who therefore should bear the financial obligations arising from it. This wider, possession-based understanding of responsibility better aligns with the practical need to ensure continuous control, proper treatment, and financial security for waste-related risks. For these reasons, the principle is more accurately expressed not as the polluter pays principle but as the waste holder pays principle, reflecting the reality that in waste management, responsibility follows possession and control rather than the act of pollution.

4 Extended Waste Producer Responsibility Principle in EU Law

As demonstrated in the preceding paragraph, the overarching concept of 'waste holder' encompasses the concept of 'waste producer'. The rule introduced by the Waste Directive refers to a producer of a product, by which the EU legislator means "any natural or legal person who professionally develops, manufactures, processes, treats, sells or imports products" (Article 8(1) of the Waste Directive). It follows from the definition that German importer of Chinese products will also be understood as a producer of a product, i.e. it is an entity that places a product on the EU market. According to this model, the producer is responsible for the entire lifecycle of the product, including the phase in which it has become waste. EPR (Extended producer responsibility) ensures that the producers bear financial and/or organizational responsibility for the management of waste. The responsibility exists from designing to manufacturing, in a way that minimizes resource consumption, to recycling and disposing a product which is easy to dismantle (recital No. 27 of the Waste Directive). Then waste is not an unwanted burden, but a profitable resource. Producers conceive and produce sustainable products, which have reduced environmental impacts and are easily recyclable.

Thinking of a product in terms of waste, the management of which is a phase in the entire lifecycle of the product, is a great and costly challenge for a manufacturer. Hence the obligation on Member States to create incentives "to encourage the design of products in order to reduce their environmental impacts and the generation of waste in the course of the production and subsequent use of products, and in order to ensure that the recovery and disposal of products that have become waste take place" (Article 8. 2 of the Waste Directive) It should be performed without endangering human health, without harming the environment. The EU legislator indicates criteria to be followed by the Member States in the implementation of the legislative or non-legislative measures to ensure that any producer of the product has extended producer responsibility. They include: 1. the technical feasibility, 2. economic viability, 3. overall environmental, human health and social impacts, 4. proper functioning of the internal market (Article 8 point 3 of the Waste Directive). According to Article 8 point of the 1 Waste Directive, "such measures may include an acceptance of returned products and of the waste that remains after those products have been used, as well as the subsequent management of the waste and financial responsibility for such activities". In addition, EPR shifts the responsibility of waste management to the producer and away from municipalities.[44]

The implementation of EPR is indeed organized at various degrees by specific directives: Directive on batteries and accumulators,[45] Directive on packaging and packaging waste,[46] Directive on end-of-life vehicles[47] and Directive on waste electrical and electronic equipment (WEEE).[48] generally relying on recovery and recycling targets laid down by legislation and constituting its ultimate goal. The principle of extended producer liability should be considered mandatory to the extent regulated by the above-mentioned directives. Due to the minimal harmonisation, states may extend this principle to other activities as well (e.g. in France).

From the point of view of this paper's topic, the example of electrical and electronic equipment producers is relevant. Under the ERP, the producer is obliged to guarantee and finance the free collection of waste electrical and electronic equipment. Small equipment (such as a hairdryer) should be collected by shops selling the producer's products. The producer is obliged to recycle waste electrical and electronic equipment at a certain percentage, which increases in accordance with EU standards. An additional financial instrument supporting the producer's

[44] Thieffry (2021), p. 260 f.

[45] Directive 2006/66/EC of the European Parliament and of the Council of 6 September 2006 on batteries and accumulators and waste batteries and accumulators and repealing Directive 91/157/EEC) OJ L 266, 26.9.2006, p. 1.

[46] European Parliament and Council Directive 94/62/EC of 20 December 1994 on packaging and packaging waste (OJ L 365, 31.12.1994, p. 10).

[47] Directive 2000/53/EC of the European Parliament and Council of 18 September 2000 on end-of life vehicles (*OJ L 269, 21.10.2000, p. 34–43*).

[48] Directive 2012/19/EU of the European Parliament and Council on waste electrical and electronic equipment [2012] OJ L197/38; https://eurlex.europa.eu/legal-content/EN/TXT/PDF/?uri=CELEX:32012L0019.

financial responsibility is the product fee, which is an alternative to meeting the standards for recycling used equipment. A producer who fails to meet the standards applicable to him is obliged to pay the product fee. Because of the risk of the producer's insolvency, the EU legislator imposes an obligation to provide financial security in case of failure to pay the product fee (more on this below).

5 Circular Economy Model and Environmental Social Governance (ESG)

The circular economy represents a production and consumption model that involves extending the life cycle of a product (referred to above). In a circular economy, the value of products, materials and resources is maintained in the economy for as long as possible, and the generation of waste is minimized. Essentially, circular economy shifts economic activity away from consumption of finite resources to sustainability. The concept is based on three core principles: design out waste and pollution; keep products and materials in use; and regenerate natural systems. This model is therefore consistent with the principle of extended producer responsibility, emphasising the continuity of the producer's responsibility throughout all stages of the product life cycle. In the context of a circular economy paradigm, the conventional distinctions between products and waste are mitigated, thereby obfuscating the conventional perception of the conclusion of a product's lifecycle.

The EU's transition from linear to a circular economy will reduce pressure on natural resources what seems to be necessary to achieve the EU's 2050 climate neutrality target[49] and to halt biodiversity damage. A circular economy will require a complete rethink of product design, the choice of materials and manufacturing processes, as well as consideration for how products can be repaired, maintained, reused and/or repurposed. The linear model to date is based on a "take-make-use-dispose" scheme: it is characterised by the use of large quantities of cheap and easily available materials and energy. Part of this model is also what is known as "planned obsolescence", i.e. designing products in such a way that they stop working after a certain period of time. It is to be replaced by a circular model based on the "repair, re-use, recycle" scheme.

In March 2020, the European Commission presented The Circular Economy Action Plan for a Cleaner and More Competitive Europe[50]—a roadmap for a circular economy, which aims to promote more sustainable product design, reduce waste and empower customers, for example by formulating a right to repair. In February

[49] The EU aims to be climate-neutral by 2050—an economy with net-zero greenhouse gas emissions - https://climate.ec.europa.eu/eu-action/climate-strategies-targets/2050-long-term-strategy_en.

[50] Communication from the Commission to the European Parliament, The Council, The European Economic and Social Committee and the Committee of the Regions: A new Circular Economy Action Plan For a cleaner and more competitive Europe COM/2020/98 final

2021, the Parliament adopted resolution on the new Circular Economy Action Plan,[51] demanding additional measures to achieve a carbon-neutral, environmentally sustainable, toxin-free and fully closed economy by 2050, including stricter recycling rules and binding targets for material use and consumption by 2030. The European Parliament has called for implementing measures to ensure that sustainable and high-quality products reach the market. Such measures aim to extend the product life cycle and keep waste to a minimum. When the product life cycle has come to an end, recycling should be the preferred method of waste management. In March 2022, the Commission published the first package of measures to accelerate the transition to a circular economy as part of the Circular Economy Action Plan In November 2022. The Commission proposed new EU packaging regulations. These aim to reduce packaging waste and improve packaging design, for example through clear labelling to promote reuse and recycling[52]; and calls for a transition to bio-based, biodegradable and compostable plastics.[53] The majority of Member States have implemented or are in the process of implementing municipal waste reforms that will result in a more circular approach and increased preparation for reuse and recycling rates in the years up to 2025 and beyond. However, in some cases, delays in applying the reforms have adverse effects on their performance. The challenges posed by the COVID-19 pandemic and the energy crisis may require specific actions to avoid delayed implementation of national waste reforms.[54]

Today, as businesses begin to design and invest in products that could be around for many decades, early engagement with insurers will be essential. The change in production and consumption patterns associated with an extended product life cycle will change insurance needs, as the role of services related to product use increases and the role of ownership decreases in favour of other rights over manufactured products.

The circular economy model has implications for the domain of insurance, as the processes of production and waste management give rise to insurance risks. The circular economy offers an opportunity to insure new activities related to product disassembly, refurbishing, and recycling. Adopting circular economy-focused practices across different industries will lead to changes in risk exposure. For example, the automotive industry is retooling its assembly lines to produce more EVs. These

[51] European Parliament resolution of 10 February 2021 on the new Circular Economy Action Plan (2020/2077(INI)).

[52] Overall, according to the assessment carried out by the European Environment Agency, the majority of Member States are at risk of missing the municipal waste preparing for re-use and recycling targets for 2025 - https://www.eea.europa.eu/publications/many-eu-member-states/many-eu-member-states-not.

[53] Proposal for a Regulation of the European Parliament and Council on packaging and packaging waste, amending Regulation (EU) 2019/1020 and Directive (EU) 2019/904, and repealing Directive 94/62/EC Brussels, 30.11.2022 COM(2022) 677 final 2022/0396 (COD).

[54] Report from the from the Commission to the European Parliament, The Council, The European Economic and Social Committee and the Committee of the Regions, Brussels, 8.6.2023 COM(2023) 304 final, p. 7.

changes to assembly lines and materials used to build the EVs could affect workers' compensation, product liability, and business interruption.

The CSRD (Corporate Sustainability Reporting Directive[55]) is a EU regulation that aims to increase the transparency of businesses on their environmental, social and governance (ESG) impacts. It introduces reporting obligations for entities with more than 250 employees and an annual turnover of more than €40 million, or assets of more than €20 million. In the longer term, the directive will also cover medium-sized and smaller enterprises.[56] In the reports, entities are required to include data on CO_2 emissions, energy efficiency, environmental impact, employee policies and management. Unlike previous requirements, CSRD reports will require external verification to ensure reliability and credibility of the presented data. The ESG audit will be conducted by independent bodies. The aim of EU regulation is to achieve greater transparency of operations through uniform reports. The transparency results in a higher awareness of counterparties' decision-making, which influences greater access to capital. The transparency achieved through detailed and verified reports also facilitates the identification of risks that hinder the realisation of the circular economy.. It is related to building their reputation as good environmental stewards.

An important issue is the link between ESG requirements and the insurance risks estimation as well as the assumption of risk by insurers.[57] As an example. Consumer protection groups requested several insurance companies, including AIG and Travelers, to underwrite high carbon-emitting firms like coal companies. This has negatively impacted those insurance companies. Insuring companies that fail to address climate change and the rising circular economy movement will be more susceptible to negative impacts on their brand and reputation among business partners and customers.

The circular economy model and ESG is also implemented on other continents. Intergovernmental organizations, including the United Nations (UN), also formed the Net-Zero Insurance Alliance in July 2021 to help the insurance industry transition to a low-carbon economy. Current members comprise nearly 30 carriers worldwide, including AXA, Swiss Re, Allianz, Munich Re, Beazley, and Zurich. The Securities and Exchange Commission (SEC) has not finalized its ESG reporting requirements for public companies in the United States. In May 2022, SEC proposed amendments to rules and reporting forms to "promote consistent, comparable, and reliable information for investors concerning funds' and advisers' incorporation of environmental, social, and governance (ESG) factors."

---

[55] DIRECTIVE (EU) 2022/2464 OF THE EUROPEAN PARLIAMENT AND OF THE COUNCIL of 14 December 2022 amending Regulation (EU) No 537/2014, Directive 2004/109/EC, Directive 2006/43/EC and Directive 2013/34/EU, as regards corporate sustainability reporting.

[56] The CSRD will take effect from 2024, with the first reports being submitted in 2025 for the 2024 financial year.

[57] Environmental Statement, EIOPA 19 September 2022, https://www.eiopa.europa.eu/system/files/2023-01/2020_environmental_statement_2022.pdf.

An important question is the extent of corporate social responsibility in relation to the responsibility of the state and its emanations. The European Parliament's accountability report emphasised that businesses must not take over the authorities task relating to promotion, performance and control of social environment protection standards. Essentially, this means that the responsibility of entrepreneurs can only reach a certain level that must not replace the role of the state. The state cannot escape responsibility by shifting it entirely onto entrepreneurs.[58]

References

Basedow J, Birds M, Clarke H, Cousy H, Heiss H, Loacker L (eds) (2016) Principles of European insurance contract law (PICL). Sellier European Law Publishers GmbH, Köln

Boomhower J (2019) Drilling like there's no tomorrow. Am Econ Rev 109(2):396

Bugge HC (2009) The polluter pays principle: dilemmas of justice in national and international contexts. In: Ebbesson J, Okowa P (eds) Environmental law and justice in context. Cambridge University Press

Colin M (2014) The regulatory potential of financial security to reduce environmental risk. J Environ Law 26:198, 201

De Sadeleer N (2010) The principles of prevention and precaution in international law: two heads of the same coin? In: Fitzmaurice M et al (eds) Research handbook on international environmental law. Edward Elgar Publishing

Dmowska J (2019) Obowiązki wytwórcy i posiadacza odpadów. In: Prawo o odpadach. Wybrane problemy, red. B. Rakoczy, Warsaw

Duvic-Paoli L-A (2018) The prevention principle in international environmental law. Cambridge University Press, Cambridge

Gniewek E, Machnikowski P (2017) Kodeks cywilny. Komentarz, Wroclaw, A. Kunicki, critical gloss on the judgment SN z 3.06.1966 r., II CR 412/68, OSPIKA 1967/10, poz. 234

Górski M (2005) Gospodarowanie odpadami w świetle prawa wspólnotowego i polskiego prawa wewnętrznego. Poznań

Landini S (2013) From environmental insurance to environmental derivatives? Eur Energy Environ Law Rev 22(6):229

Malinowska K (2024) Prevention in environmental insurance. In: Malinowska K, Maśniak D (eds) Managing environmental risk through insurance. Springer Nature, pp 283–299

Maśniak D (2021) Wykorzystanie ubezpieczeń do naprawy szkód w środowisku o rozmiarach katastrofalnych, Prawo Morskie tom XL, Gdańsk

Noussia K (2023) Global offshore energy installations: implications for environmental pollution liability insurance in relation to major oil spill incidents. Eur Energy Environ Law Rev 32

Peel J (2005) The precautionary principle in practice; Environmental decision-making. Scientific Uncertainty, The Federation Press, Sydney

Sangowski T (ed) (2001) Ubezpieczenia Gospodarcze. Warsaw

Skowrońska-Bocian E, Warciński M (2020) In: Pietrzykowski K (ed) Kodeks cywilny Tom I. Komentarz do art. 1–449. Warsaw 2020, art. 336, nb. 2

Thieffry P (2021) Handbook of European environmental and climate law, 2nd edn. Larcier

[58] Report – A7-0023/2013, European Parliament. Report on Corporate Social Responsibility: promoting society's interests and a route to sustainable and inclusive recovery, https://www.europarl.europa.eu/doceo/document/A-7-2013-0023_EN.html, 20. Dec.2020.).

Insurance as a Type of Financial Security

1 Introduction

The considerations developed in Chapter III sought to examine the extent of the legislator's intervention in different forms of waste management that give rise to environmental risks, with particular emphasis on the legal architecture governing financial security mechanisms. That analysis revealed not only the diversity of regulatory approaches across the various sectoral directives, but also the practical significance of issues such as the identification of the competent authority responsible for determining the amount and form of financial security. These findings demonstrate that the normative role of financial security extends far beyond its strictly economic function and must be assessed through the lens of its legal nature.

In order to provide a comprehensive response to the question of whether insurance may serve as an adequate instrument of financial security in this context, it is necessary to engage more deeply with the doctrinal foundations of financial security, in particular its classification as a form of personal security. Since the prevailing regulatory practice tends to equate insurance with the insurance contract, the present chapter focuses on insurance in this form and examines whether such a contract may properly fulfill the function imposed by environmental legislation.

Accordingly, the chapter undertakes a systematic comparison between the insurance contract and other legally recognized forms of financial security—such as bank guarantees, surety bonds and trust-based mechanisms—in order to assess their respective suitability for securing the performance of environmental obligations. The aim is to determine whether insurance can operate as an effective legal instrument within the framework of ecological waste management and, if so, to delineate the scope and limitations of its applicability. Such an inquiry is essential not only for understanding the current regulatory landscape, but also for identifying the conceptual and doctrinal adjustments that may be required to ensure that insurance, where appropriate, can function as a coherent and legally sound form of financial security.

D. Maśniak, *The Legal Framework for the Use of Insurance in Ecological Waste Management*, AIDA Europe Research Series on Insurance Law and Regulation 17, https://doi.org/10.1007/978-3-032-26550-0_4

2 EU Mandatory Financial Security Requirements

2.1 The Purpose and Scope

The main EU legislation that includes mandatory financial security provisions regulating environmental responsibilities for waste are the Landfill Directive,[1] the Extractive Waste Directive,[2] the Waste Shipments Regulation, the Directive on waste electrical and electronic equipment. Eighteen Member States (Belgium, Croatia, Cyprus, the Czech Republic, Denmark, Estonia, France, Germany, Greece, Hungary, Ireland, Italy, Latvia, Lithuania, the Netherlands, Poland, Croatia and Spain) have introduced mandatory financial security that goes beyond EU requirements for activities associated with waste. V. Fogleman points out that there are two main types of environmental financial security requirements: financial security for environmental responsibilities; and financial security for environmental liabilities. The above EU requirements, however, all refer to financial security for environmental responsibilities. The implementation of EU regulations has led to a situation where the national legislation goes beyond the EU law. In some cases, the national legislation includes requirements for financial security for environmental responsibilities and environmental liabilities.

From the point of view of EU environmental requirements as a social interest per se, first type of financial security for environmental responsibilities (such as closing a landfill or post-mining reclamation) is crucial. Importantly, this type of financial security involves a leading role of the regulatory authority which decides about eventual closure or restoration of such a site. It is difficult to agree that closure or remediation costs are estimated before they occur. However, it must be accepted that the design of the financial security required of the waste holder at the stage of undertaking an activity (landfill management, waste collection or waste treatment) requiring a permit from an environmental/regulatory authority tends towards this.[3]

Prior to operating a landfill site, the holder of waste shall provide the regulatory authority with information on the extent and nature of its activities. Financial security allows an environmentally risky activity to be undertaken without requiring the waste holder to pay the full amount of the estimated costs. Financial security other than a security deposit reconciles the conflicting interests of the profit-seeking start-up entrepreneur on the one hand, and the regulatory authority representing the public on the other. Even if the required financial security relates to estimated costs to be covered, by agreeing these with the regulatory authority they can be determined as certain, which influences the choice of financial security (more on this below).

---

[1] Council Directive 1999/31/EC on the landfill of waste [1999] OJ L182/1; https://eur-lex.europa.eu/legalcontent/EN/TXT/?uri=CELEX:31999L0031.

[2] Council Directive 2016/21/EC on the management of waste from extractive industries [2016] OJ L102/15; https://eur-lex.europa.eu/legal-content/EN/TXT/?uri=CELEX:02006L0021-20090807.

[3] Fogleman (2023), pp. 55–60.

The second type is financial security for liabilities which relates to an unknown and unforeseen event, such as a pollution incident or other event that may never occur. Valerie Fogleman points out that in this case it is not possible to estimate the amount of the required financial security with as much accuracy as in the case of financial security for responsibilities. Whereas it is possible to estimate the cost of environmental responsibilities by reference to, say, the amount of waste at a landfill, it is more difficult to estimate the cost of environmental liabilities.

The amount of financial security may follow from the legislation or is left to the discretion of the regulatory authority. Polish Waste Act[4] is an example of a regulation specifying the amount of financial security. According to this act, the amount is calculated as the product of the largest mass of waste that could be stored in an installation, a construction facility or a part thereof, or a waste storage area, taking into account the dimensions of the construction facility or a part thereof, or another waste storage area, and the rate of the security of claims resulting from the regulation of the Minister of the Environment.[5]The amount of security depends on the size and nature of the waste holder's activities, the probability of environmental damage and the existence of an environmental management system. An alternative approach is to base the amount of financial security on the probable costs of depollution or reparation of other environmental damage—an ad hoc basis or on a worst case basis.[6]

Eighteen member states (Belgium (for soil remediation), Croatia, Cyprus, the Czech Republic, Denmark (for oil tank remediation), Estonia, Finland (for compensation only), France, Germany, Greece, Hungary, Ireland, Italy, Latvia, Lithuania, the Netherlands, Poland, Spain) have introduced mandatory security requirements for waste management operations. These requirements range from financial securities for various waste operations to financial securities for waste remediation in other countries, notably Belgium and the Netherlands. Some of the requirements apply to civil liabilities for damage caused by waste; others apply to reclamation, disposal or other handling of waste.[7]

Some member states have introduced mandatory financial security for certain civil liabilities, i.e. claims for personal injury and property damage related to waste management. These include Croatia (waste management permits, including permits for landfills and extractive waste facilities), the Czech Republic (landfills), Greece (civil liability claims against holders of permits for the transportation of hazardous waste or for handling, storage, disposal or recovery of hazardous waste at operator sites), Italy (certain waste operators in the Veneto region), Lithuania (hazardous waste management operators), Poland (operators of carbon dioxide landfills) and Spain (hazardous waste treatment sites).

---

[4] The Act of 14 December 2012 on waste (Polish Journal of Laws of 2018, item 992 as amended).

[5] Ordinance of the Minister of Environment of 3 February 2019 concerning the rates of security of claims (Polish Journal of Laws of 2019, item 256).

[6] Cf. Fogleman (2023), p. 82.

[7] V. Fogleman, ibidem.

For example, legislation in Greece requires a business that manages hazardous waste to have mandatory financial security. Most of the demand for environmental insurance policies there comes from businesses that are subject to this requirement.[8]

2.2 *The Landfill*

The Landfill Directive was adopted to prevent or mitigate the negative effects on the environment from landfilling waste as much as possible. Each landfill shall be classified in one of the following classes: landfill for hazardous waste, landfill for non-hazardous waste, landfill for inert waste (Article 4). In addition, according to the preamble to that directive (no 19) "in each case, checks should be made to establish whether the waste may be placed in the landfill for which it is intended, in particular as regards hazardous waste". The Directive does this, among other things, by: (a) requiring hazardous waste, non-hazardous waste and inert waste to be disposed of in separate landfills; (b) specifying the types of waste that may not be disposed of in landfills; (c) banning the landfilling of waste that does not meet certain waste acceptance criteria; and (d) requiring landfills to meet technical and financial security requirements.

The Landfill Directive requires an operator to have financial security to meet the closure and post closure obligations under the permit. Article 8(a)(iv) of the Landfill Directive directs Member States to take measures so that the competent authorities do not issue a permit for a landfill unless they are satisfied, among other things, that: "adequate provisions, by way of a financial security or any other equivalent, on the basis of modalities to be decided by Member States, has been or will be made by the applicant prior to the commencement of disposal operations to ensure that the obligations (including after-care provisions) arising under the permit … are discharged and that the closure procedures required by [the Landfill Directive] are followed. This security or its equivalent shall be kept as long as required by maintenance and after-care operation of the site in accordance with [the Landfill Directive]". This wording relates the conditions of the financial security to the conditions of the landfill permit. The purpose of the security is to finance the consequences of failing to comply with the requirements imposed by the administrative authority, including the closure procedure for the landfill site.

The Member States have been obliged to "take measures to ensure that all of the costs involved in the setting up and operation of a landfill site, including as far as possible the cost of the financial security or its equivalent referred to in Article 8(a)(iv), and the estimated costs of the closure and after-care of the site for a period of at least 30 years shall be covered by the price to be charged by the operator for the disposal of any type of waste in that site" (Article 10 Landfill Directive). Such an obligation can be understood as a requirement for the state (executive authority or

[8] Ibidem.

legislature power) to support the operator of disposal in its activities (waste purchase) due to the significant costs of this undertaking, including the cost of financial security. It is important in the context of the problem of illegal landfills, particularly hazardous waste landfills. The question arises as to whether their existence (e.g. around 400 illegal landfills in Poland in 2023[9]) is not due to overly stringent financial requirements resulting in waste being abandoned in places not intended for it.[10] On the other hand, one should remember that according to the EU's waste hierarchy, landfilling is the least preferable option and should be limited to the necessary minimum.

Some of Member States began introducing legislation concerning a problem of hazardous waste in the early 1980s, following the discovery of contaminated sites, especially in Denmark, the Netherlands, and Sweden. In Denmark, a waste dump was discovered that was leaching approximately five tonnes of mercury and other chemicals into the sea at Harboøre Tange.[11] In the Netherlands, hazardous waste was discovered at residential areas in Lekkerkerk and Gouderak.[12] In Sweden, a waste dump at Skåne that contained approximately 800 barrels of hazardous waste was discovered.[13] The Swedish Environmental Code has a general rule on financial security that applies to all permits, approvals or exemptions pursuant to the Code (including the Landfill Directive). According to section 3 of Chapter 16: "The validity of a permit, approval or exemption may be made subject to the requirement that the person who intends to pursue the activity must furnish a security for the costs of after-treatment and any other restoration measures that may be necessary as a result". The type of security shall be governed by chapter 2, section 25 of the Enforcement Code as a pledge or financial guarantee. Securities shall be examined by the licensing authority and lodged with the county administrative board.

Financial security under the Landfill Directive operates as a regulatory tool of environmental governance, ensuring that operators cannot externalise the long-term environmental risks inherent in waste disposal activities, particularly onto society, represented by public authorities. It provides a legally mandated safety net that secures the financial resources necessary to address the consequences of non-compliance with permit obligations, thereby supporting both deterrence and

[9] Ociepa-Kicińska (2023), pp. 570–583.

[10] For more on the problem of illegal landfills, see Vaverková et al. (2019).

[11] Church and Nakamura (1994), pp. 41–42; Ministry of the Environment, 'Soil Contamination: Solution to the Cheminova toxic waste dump problem' Danish Environment Newsletter No. 28 (December 2003).

[12] See Paul Lewis, 'Following U.S., Europe Awakens to the Dangers of Toxic Wastes' New York Times (20 February 1983) http://www.nytimes.com/1983/02/20/weekinreview/following-us-europe-awakens-to-the-dangers-of-toxic-wastes.html (access 10.05.2023); see also Betlem (1995), p. 294.

[13] See Paul Lewis, 'Following U.S., Europe Awakens to the Dangers of Toxic Wastes' New York Times (20 February 1983) http://www.nytimes.com/1983/02/20/weekinreview/following-us-europe-awakens-to-the-dangers-of-toxic-wastes.html (access 10.05.2023); Baltic Environment and Energy, Swedish Environmental Policies, History and present regulations (Report 3 of the BEE project, 2007) 5; see also Fogleman (2015), pp. 42–61.

effective environmental restoration. Its practical effectiveness, however, depends on achieving a careful balance between ensuring adequate coverage of environmental liabilities and maintaining economic feasibility, so as not to inadvertently encourage illegal disposal practices that the Directive seeks to prevent. In this context, the specific form of financial security—such as insurance contract or insurance guarantees—is of considerable importance, a matter that will be examined in the subsequent chapters.

2.3 *Extractive Waste*

The extraction and processing of minerals generates a considerable amount of waste. The majority of mining waste includes gangue or tailings. Some of these wastes are inert and therefore do not cause significant pollution. However, some waste products may contain large quantities of dangerous substances, such as heavy metals, or cause acid or alkaline drainage. The environmental impact of a mine can be particularly significant if the leaching of these dangerous substances reaches the groundwater, lakes, rivers, or other bodies of water.[14] Therefore, to prevent and reduce the adverse effects of mines, mining operators are responsible for managing waste in a manner which is sustainable in the long term.

For the foreseeable future in both emerging and developed countries, mining has emerged as the most urgent global sustainability issue of the modern era.[15] Today, the storage and management of the large quantities of waste generated by the mineral processing is already a major issue. One type of such waste, a fine-grained mineral sand called tailings, is often stored in heaps or ponds surrounded by high embankment dams. For example, the potential failure of a tailings dam could have catastrophic consequences, as it did in Aznalcóllar (Spain, 1998) as well as Baia Mare and Baia Borsa (Romania, 2000) to name a few.[16] Mining waste can pose an environmental hazard long after the mine closure, and because of the severity of potential impacts, it is crucial that these waste facilities are properly managed. Proper management ensures the long-term safety of these facilities as well as minimising water and soil pollution. The mining sector is governed through legislations with fundamentally different functions. On one hand, mining operators are granted concession by laws which are meant to facilitate the exploitation of mineral resources. On the other hand, environmental laws are designed to limit or prohibit certain harmful activities, and to impose obligations on the operators through permit procedures and other generally applicable rules. Nations around the world are faced with the problem of establishing efficient financial assurance programmes that

[14] Swedish Environmental Protection Agency, Förhållandet mellan minerallagen och miljöbalken, pp. 12–13.

[15] Hosseinpour (2022), Article 132955.

[16] Owen et al. (2020), tom 42, s. 2–3.

require mining operators to provide financial guarantee in case of mine closure.[17] It also applies to Europe.

A mining operation not only involves the extraction and processing of minerals, but also the management of extractive waste. Therefore, in practice, the mining waste management and the mining itself are carried out by the same operator. The operator must plan and carry out their operations in a way that minimises all damage caused to the property. However, not all damages can be averted, because thorough exploration often involves drilling for samples or digging trenches. The operator is liable for any damages caused by their activities.[18] Therefore, to prevent and reduce the adverse effects of mines, mining operators are responsible for managing mining waste in a manner which is sustainable in the long term.[19] To ensure that this obligation is fulfilled, the operator is required to lodge a financial guarantee before the operation commences. The guarantee is designed to provide the necessary funds for environment remediation, even in the event of the operator's bankruptcy. Thus, the financial guarantee alleviates the risk that the state would have to bear the costs for remediation. The adequacy of this guarantee is examined by the same authority as in the environmental permitting process and held by the regulatory authority.

The purpose of the Extractive Waste Directive (also called the Mining Waste Directive) is, as stated by article 1 of the Directive, to provide for "measures, procedures and guidance to prevent or reduce as far as possible any adverse effects on the environment, in particular water, air, soil, fauna and flora and landscape, and any resultant risks to human health, brought about as a result of the management of waste from the extractive industries". Recital 25 states, among other things, that operators of extractive waste facilities must: "lodge a financial guarantee or equivalent in accordance with procedures to be decided by the Member States ensuring that all the obligations flowing from the permit will be fulfilled, including those relating to the closure and after-closure of the waste facility. The financial guarantee should be sufficient to cover the cost of rehabilitation of the land affected by the waste facility, which includes the waste facility itself, as described in the waste management plan prepared … and required by the … permit, by a suitably qualified and independent third party". The Directive requires an operator to have financial security for obligations arising from the permit, including post-closure measures and the rehabilitation of land affected by the waste facility.

The Commission issued technical guidelines on financial security pursuant to the Extractive Waste Directive.[20] The guidelines stipulate that Member States shall base calculation of the financial guarantee for the waste facility on the following: "a) its

---

[17] Twum (2013), pp. 200–208.

[18] This is, for example, provided for in Article 7 1-3 of Swedish Mineral Act.

[19] This is, for example, provided for in Article 15:35, 16:3 of Swedish Environmental Code.

[20] Commission Decision on technical guidelines for the establishment of the financial guarantee in accordance with Directive 2006/21/EC of the European Parliament and of the Council concerning the management of waste from extractive industries OJ L101/25; https://eur-lex.europa.eu/legal-content/EN/TXT/PDF/?uri=CELEX:32009D0335&from=EN.

likely impacts on human health and the environment; b) the definition of rehabilitation including its after use; c) applicable environmental standards and objectives, including physical stability of the waste facility, minimum quality standards for the soil and water resources and maximum release rates of contaminants; d) technical measures required to achieve environmental objectives, especially measures aimed at ensuring the stability of the facility and limiting environmental damage; e) measures required to achieve objectives during and after closure, including land rehabilitation, after closure treatment and monitoring if required, and, if relevant, measures to reinstate biodiversity; f) the estimated time scale of impacts and required mitigation measures; and g) an assessment of the costs necessary to ensure land rehabilitation, closure and after closure including possible monitoring or treatment of contaminants".

In Sweden, around 75% of all waste is generated by the mining sector. Sweden's position as a leading country in both supporting mining and setting environmental standards makes it undoubtedly an interesting and useful case study of mine waste and the remediation of mining activities. In accordance with provisions of the Swedish Environmental Code (§ 36 a,b), permits for mining operations which are subject to requirements for a mine waste-management plan must incorporate an obligation for a mining business to provide financial collateral for meeting its responsibilities. When ruling on permits for mining or mining facilities for extraction, exploration, processing, or enrichment, the Land and Environment Court must obtain an initial statement from the Debt Office on the calculation of the size of the collateral and a second statement on the acceptance of the collateral.

The Mining Waste Directive requires an operator, as the holder of mining waste, to maintain financial security covering the liabilities arising from the mining permit, including post-closure obligations and the rehabilitation of areas affected by the operation of the facility. This establishes a mechanism ensuring the availability of financial resources collected through instruments provided by financial market entities. The objective of this mechanism is to safeguard public funds that would otherwise have to be used in the event of the operator's insolvency. As in the other EU instruments discussed in this chapter, this mechanism is implemented through financial instruments, among which insurance constitutes a significant component.

2.4 The Shipments of Waste

The Shipments of Waste Regulation implements the Basel Convention[21] and the OECD Decision on the control of transboundary movements of waste[22] in the EU. The Regulation lays down procedures for transboundary shipments of waste within the EU and between Member States and third countries, including a ban on the export of waste for disposal. The Article 5.8 of the Regulation states, among other things, that a financial guarantee or equivalent insurance must be established and declared in the notification for the shipment of waste. Article 5.8 further provides that the financial guarantee or equivalent insurance shall be submitted as part of the notification document before the shipment starts. Article 7 sets out requirements for the financial guarantee or equivalent insurance. It must cover "1) the costs of transport, 2) recovery or disposal including any necessary interim operations, and 3) storage of the waste for 90 days". Article 7(2) states that the intent of the financial guarantee or equivalent insurance is to provide "for the shipment or recovery of the waste when they cannot be completed as intended" or "the shipment, recovery or disposal is illegal". According to Article 7(5), the financial guarantee or equivalent insurance shall be valid for and cover a notified shipment and completion of recovery or disposal of the notified waste. The distinction between a financial guarantee and insurance is noteworthy. Such a provision suggests that the legislator does not see an insurance guarantee as part of the broader concept of insurance. Moreover, it is not clear why an insurance contract is not treated as a financial guarantee, and requires an explicit reference through the use of a conjunction ("and equivalent insurance").

The specificity and importance of the risks associated with shipments of waste is underlined by the choice of legal measure made by the EU legislator. Unlike other normative acts on waste management, this is a regulation, that is an act with direct effect. This means that, in this area, the legislator limits the freedom of Member States to use national legal measures for implementation. The decision to regulate transboundary shipments of waste through a directly applicable regulation further highlights the sensitivity and gravity of the risks involved, limiting Member States' discretion and ensuring uniform application of financial security requirements across the EU. In 2010, a Commission study was conducted to provide an analysis of the practices in the Member States with regard to the financial guarantee or equivalent insurance as set out in Article 6 of The Shipments of Waste Regulation. The correspondents, pursuant to Article 54 of Regulation (EC) No 1013/2006 on

---

[21] Basel Convention on the Control of Transboundary Movements of Hazardous Wastes and Their Disposal Protocol on Liability and Compensation for Damage Resulting from Transboundary Movements of Hazardous Wastes and their Disposal, texts and annexes revised in 2019, 2020.

[22] OECD, Decision of the Council C(2001)107/Final concerning the control of transboundary movements of wastes destined for recovery operations as amended by C(2004)20; Decision of the Council C(2001)107/Final concerning the control of transboundary movements of wastes destined for recovery operations; the consolidated version of 14 June 2001 [C/M(2001)13] and of 28 February 2002 [C/M(2002)4].

shipments of waste (WSR), agreed that there is no need to develop a common European method for the calculation of the financial guarantee or equivalent insurance.[23] The new regulation on shipments of waste includes a new provision (Article 7.10), according to which: "The Commission shall assess the feasibility of establishing a simple, risk-based and harmonised calculation method for determining the amount of financial guarantees or equivalent insurances and, if appropriate, adopt an implementing act to establish such a simple, risk-based and harmonised calculation method". In the second subparagraph, the EU legislator highlighted the role of "relevant rules of the Member States relating to the calculation of the financial guarantee or equivalent insurance", which the Commision shall take into account in carrying out the assessment referred to in the first subparagraph. This demonstrates a shift toward greater coherence and potential standardisation, while still recognising the diversity of national practices.

In accordance with the Waste Shipments Regulation, the requirement to establish a financial guarantee or equivalent insurance functions as a regulatory mechanism for controlling the transboundary movement of waste. The Regulation mandates that such security be constituted and submitted prior to the commencement of any notified shipment, reflecting the legislator's intention to ensure that the waste holder is able to bear the financial burden of the environmental risks associated with transport, including risks arising during recovery or disposal operations, thereby shielding public authorities from the need to deploy public funds. Notwithstanding the uncertainties surrounding the legislator's choice of the alternative formulation "financial guarantee or equivalent insurance," it is important to underscore the explicit recognition of insurance as, in the legislator's view, an appropriate form of financial security.

2.5 *Waste Electrical and Electronic (E-Waste)*

The EU adopted the Waste Electrical and Electronic Directive to improve the collection, treatment and recycling of waste electrical and electronic equipment (WEEE). Article 8(3) of the WEEE Directive obligates Member States to ensure that producers or third parties acting on their behalf establish systems to provide for the recovery of WEEE using best available techniques. The systems may be established by producers individually or collectively.

Article 12(3) states that the guarantee may take "the form of participation by the producer in appropriate schemes for the financing of the management of WEEE, a recycling insurance or a blocked bank account". Recital 23 states that the purpose of the requirement is "to prevent costs for the management of WEEE from orphan products from falling on society or the remaining producers". Most Member States

[23] Method of Calculation in the Member States of the Financial Guarantee and Equivalent Insurance pursuant to Art. 6 of Regulation (EC) No 1013/2006 on shipments of waste - A Compilation Document - https://environment.ec.europa.eu/topics/waste-and-recycling/waste-shipments_en.

have established compliance schemes to satisfy the requirement for a financial guarantee—"appropriate schemes for the financing of the management of WEEE". The compliance schemes also enable producers to meet other requirements of the WEEE Directive. As a result, most producers of WEEE did not get bank instruments or purchase insurance protection.[24]

The solutions adopted by Poland are an interesting example of the implementation of the WEEE Directive.[25] Producers who launch of household appliances have been obliged to provide financial security for a given calendar year to cover the product fee (Article 27 of the Act). The financial security may take the form of a bank deposit or an insurance guarantee. Thus, a potential public law liability for a payable product fee has been linked with a private financial guarantee instrument. A producer of equipment who launches of household appliances is obliged to organise and finance the waste equipment collection from the distributors collecting waste equipment, and finance the recycling process of these wastes (Article 18) at a certain level.

A producer of equipment who has not fulfilled the obligation to achieve the minimum annual level of waste equipment collection, level of recovery or level of preparing for reuse and recycling, is obliged to pay a product fee, calculated separately for each group of equipment, if the required level is not achieved: (1) collection; (2) recovery; (3) preparation for reuse and recycling (Article 72 of the Act). The product fee constitutes a public levy that goes to the voivodeship budget. In case of a producer of equipment who launches of household appliances has not attained the required minimum annual level of waste equipment collection, level of recovery or level of preparing for reuse and recycling, and has not paid a product fee, the province marshal rules, by way of a decision, that funds from the financial security are allocated to cover the product fee (Article 33 section 2).

The requirement for a financial guarantee introduced under the WEEE Directive differs from the previously discussed EU instruments, which link financial security obligations to the commencement of specific waste-related activities by certain categories of waste holders. In the case of the WEEE Directive, the mechanism is designed to incentivise recycling as the preferred waste management option. The Polish approach exemplifies a model that combines private financial instruments, such as insurance, with public financial instruments, including obligatory fees. With appropriate legislative support, this hybrid model can provide an effective alternative for achieving environmental objectives.

[24] Fogleman (2020), p. 117.

[25] Act of 11 September 2015 on Waste Electrical and Electronic Equipment (Polish Journal of Laws of 2024, item 573).

2.6 *Financial Security V. Principle of Limited Liability*

The doctrine of limited liability is a fundamental principle of company law. In the case of limited liability, a person's financial liability does not exceed the amount invested in the limited liability company. Instead, companies are considered to be legal entities separate from their owners and shareholders. This means that their liabilities are also separate. As the individual owner's financial liability is limited, there is no risk of their assets being confiscated if the company fails to meet its financial obligations. Consequently, there is limited availability of capital which facilitates investment and economic development.[26] However, in the context of environmental protection, limited liability has also been identified as one of the sources of environmental and financial irresponsibility. The cost of repairing environmental damage often exceeds the polluter's ability to pay. However, shareholders can profit from a company and still avoid its debts, including clean-up costs, if it goes bankrupt. Limited liability may also encourage shareholders to withdraw capital from the company and then take environmental and/or financial action.[27]

The principle of limited liability[28] which is favourable to shareholders, may lead to the ineffectiveness of claims against the waste holder due to its insolvency. This is particularly probable in case of closure of waste facility by the operator, often linked to the financial health of the company.

On some occasions, an operator cannot fulfil their environmental obligations because of the company's bankruptcy. It is in the state's best interest to take the necessary measures to prevent further environmental damage and to even take restorative measures for environment rehabilitation. The costs of rehabilitation can be substantial, and to prevent the taxpayers from bearing them, the legislatures in Europe have developed solutions to circumvent the doctrine of limited liability.[29] The financial guarantee instrument was the most important of these solutions, and is meant to ensure that the operator fulfils the environmental obligations even in the event of its bankruptcy.[30]

2.7 *The Amount of Financial Security and State Aid*

Imposing financial security by the EU legislation is intended to involve private resources, particularly from the financial market, in financing the social objectives, which certainly include environmental protection. Requiring Member States to

---

[26] Ireland (2010), pp. 845–847.

[27] Dent (1991), pp. 151–182, 1.

[28] See more broadly Ireland (2010), pp. 837–856.

[29] Bocken (2009), pp. 146–151.

[30] Maunumäki (2020), p. 10.

incentivise the use of private sources of financing is intended to protect public funds, particularly including budgetary funds.

Incentives, which in their most stringent form are compulsory financial securities, were designed to prevent state aid or limit it to the necessary level. Such solutions, aiming at greater involvement of business in achieving the social objectives, are also characteristic of other EU regulations dealing with problems of a social nature, such as the protection of agricultural crops[31] or the road accident victims protection.[32]The Court of Justice ruling T-257/18 Iberpotash SA v European Commission is particularly relevant in the context of the role played by financial security in preventing the granting of unlawful State aid within the EU. The case concerned a Spanish mining operator which had obtained an environmental permit for the extraction of potash. As part of the permit obligations, the operator was required to provide a financial guarantee to ensure the implementation of the rehabilitation plan for the mining site. However, the amount of this guarantee was found by the Tribunal Superior de Justicia de Cataluña to be significantly lower than what would have been necessary to cover the actual restoration costs. This assessment was upheld by the Tribunal Supremo, which confirmed that the financial guarantee had been set at an insufficient level. Subsequently, on 17 December 2007, the Ministerio de Medio Ambiente and the Agencia Catalana del Agua entered into an agreement to finance the covering of the Vilafruns waste heap—an intervention which, in practice, substituted for the inadequate level of the financial guarantee originally imposed on Iberpotash.

The European Commission considered both the inadequately low level of the guarantee and the public financing of the waste heap restoration as constituting State aid.[33] In its decision, the Commission held that the excessively low amount of the guarantee resulted in disproportionately low guarantee fees. This provided Iberpotash with an economic advantage compared to operators who would have been required to bear the full market cost of an appropriately calculated financial security. The Commission therefore identified two aid measures: (1) State aid granted through reduced guarantee fees, resulting from the unduly low level of the guarantees; (2) State aid relating to the investment covering the Vilafruns waste heap, which exceeded the maximum aid intensity permitted for environmental protection.

---

[31] The EU legislator provided for "financial contributions to premiums for crop, animal and plant insurance against economic losses to farmers cause by adverse climatic events, animal or plant diseases, pest infestation, or an environmental incident" (Article 36 section 1 of Regulation (EU) No 1305/2013, 1307/2013 and 1308/2013) The conditions for support under Article 36 Section 1(a) are regulated in Article 37 of the above-mentioned Regulation. EU subsidies for insurance premiums are still under-utilised and not many farmers benefited from them. European Court of Auditors, under Regulations (EU) No 1305/2013, (EU) No 1307/2013 and (EU) No 1308/2013.

[32] See more broadly Maśniak (2016).

[33] Commission Decision (EU) 2018/118 of 31 August 2017 on State aid SA.35818 (2016/C) (ex 2015/NN) (ex 2012/CP) implemented by Spain for Iberpotash (OJ 2018 L 28, p. 25).

The significance of the Iberpotash judgment for the present discussion lies in the fact that the Court accepted the Commission's reasoning that the amount of the financial guarantee itself may determine whether an operator is obtaining an economic advantage from the State. The case demonstrates that an insufficiently high guarantee does not merely weaken environmental protection but may also distort competition by reducing an operator's compliance costs and, consequently, by conferring a selective benefit prohibited under Article 107 TFEU.

Thus, the ruling confirms that the adequacy of the financial guarantee is a legally relevant factor: if the guarantee is set below the actual costs necessary to ensure proper rehabilitation, the operator is relieved of expenses that it would normally be required to bear under market conditions. This principle supports the conclusion drawn by environmental experts that, under Royal Decree 975/2009,[34] "the amount of the financial guarantee should definitely not be lower than the basic costs of restoration".[35] The Iberpotash case therefore provides a jurisprudential foundation for the expectation that the level of financial security must correspond to real environmental liabilities in order to avoid the grant of unlawful State aid.

The ruling discussed above concerns the important dilemma of the scope of discretion for administrative authorities in determining the amount of required financial security. The EU legislator is very cautious in imposing requirements on Member States in this respect, limiting itself to wording such as *the financial guarantee should be sufficient to cover the cost of rehabilitation of the land affected by the waste facility* (recital 27 of Extractive Waste Directive), while at the same time seeking clarification of requirements by Member States in this area, as evidenced by the Commission's technical guidelines on financial security pursuant to the Extractive Waste Directive. The only change related to financial security in the new The Shipment Directive can be regarded as the most far-reaching interference of the EU legislator in this respect. According to the aforementioned Article 7.10, "The Commission shall assess the feasibility of establishing a simple, risk-based and harmonised calculation method for determining the amount of financial guarantees or equivalent insurances" considering "relevant rules of the Member States relating to the calculation of the financial guarantee or equivalent insurance". The problem arises from the conflicting interests –the interest of the private entrepreneur who is also the holder of waste that threatens the environment as a common good (public interest). In this case, there is also a conflict of public interests which include environmental protection and economic development that conditions the well-being of society. In the case of the mining operator, their activities are linked to securing the need for heat. The financial security is an operating cost for the entrepreneur. It needs to be balanced so that it disincentivise entrepreneurs from landfilling as it is the least environmentally sound form of waste management. At the same time, it

---

[34] Royal Decree 975/2009'). According to First Transitory Disposition (Disposición transitoria primera) of the Royal Decree 975/2009, the provisions of that act concerning the financial guarantees.

[35] Ibidem, p. 34.

does not encourage illegal landfilling or transport because of overly strict requirements.

An example of this is the draft amendment to Polish national regulations[36] which are a way of implementing the Landfill Directive. The drafters requested a change to Article 48a) of the Waste Act, which reads: "The amount of security for claims shall be calculated as the product of the largest mass of waste that could be stored in the installation, a construction facility or a part thereof, or a waste storage area, taking into account the dimensions of the construction facility or a part thereof, or another storage area, and the rate of the security of claims" by replacing the word "product" with "half of the product". The proposed change was justified by competition protection, emphasising that this method of calculating the amount of financial security prevents small and medium-sized enterprises from conducting business activity.

It remains unclear which authority should ultimately be responsible for determining the amount of financial security. The question arises as to the extent to which this assessment should fall within the discretion of the competent environmental authority, and to what extent national or EU legislators should intervene in order to ensure legal certainty and consistency. Although the determination of financial security is inherently case-specific and therefore unlikely to be suitable for full harmonisation at the EU level, the need to prevent unlawful State aid and distortions of competition requires Member States to establish transparent, objective and verifiable criteria for calculating its amount. Such criteria must, of course, respect the primacy of environmental protection and the principles of EU law, yet they also need to remain proportionate and operable in practice, bearing in mind that waste holders do not constitute a homogeneous group of economic operators and may be affected differently by uniformly applied financial burdens.

3 US Mandatory Financial Security

3.1 Hazardous Waste Transportation

The Motor Carrier Act 1980[37] was introduced by the federal government. Among other things, the Act requires commercial businesses that transport 'oil', 'hazardous materials', 'hazardous substances' and 'hazardous waste' to have evidence of financial security. They have been defined as "hazardous" by reference to whether they are "capable of posing an unreasonable risk to health, safety and property when transported in commerce". The damages covered by the financial security are "public liability, property damage, and environmental restoration". The regulations

[36] Bill amending the act on amendments to certain acts aimed at removing administrative and legal barriers, Polish Sejm paper 2628.

[37] 49 United States Code ss 31131 *et seq.*

define the term "environmental restoration" as: "restitution for the loss, damage, or destruction of natural resources arising out of the accidental discharge, dispersal, release or escape into or upon the land, atmosphere, watercourse, or body of water of any commodity transported by a motor carrier. This shall include the cost of removal and the cost of necessary measure taken to minimize or mitigate damage to human health, the natural environment, fish, shellfish, and wildlife".[38]

A carrier may provide evidence of financial security by insurance, a guarantee, a surety bond issued by a bonding company authorised to do business in the US, or qualification as a self-insurer.[39]

3.2 *Hazardous and Non-hazardous Waste Management*

Owners and operators of hazardous waste TSDFs (treatment, storage and disposal facilities) and hazardous waste management units (HWMUs; such as containers, tanks, containment buildings, waste piles and surface storage facilities) are subject to both environmental liability and environmental responsibility requirements.[40]

The owner or operator of a TSDF or HWMU shall possess sufficient financial resources for the closure and post-closure, which are considered environmental responsibility requirements.[41] Activities to be carried out during the closure include closing the TSDF or HWMU, removing all waste from it, decontaminating or removing equipment, and cleaning the surrounding soil. Activities to be carried out in the post-closure include monitoring, record keeping and other long-term maintenance activities for at least 30 years after closure.[42] If the owner or operator of an HWMU closes the unit in accordance with "clean closure" requirements, including closure of tanks, surface storage areas and removal of waste piles, then the evidence of financial security for post-closure activities is not required. There is no need for such financial security, as all waste and contamination would be removed from the unit and the surrounding soil.

The owner or operator of a TSDF or HWMU that is not owned by the federal or state government may provide proof of financial security through the following instruments: trust fund; a payment or performance guarantee together with a reserve trust fund; an irrevocable letter of credit together with a reserve trust fund; and insurance policy.[43] The amount of required financial security is based on the

---

[38] 49 Code of Federal Regulations s 387.5.

[39] 49 United States Code s 31139(f)(1).

[40] US Environmental Protection Agency, Financial Assurance Requirements for Hazardous Waste Treatment, Storage and Disposal Facilities; https://www.epa.gov/hwpermitting/financial-assurance-requirements-hazardous-waste-treatment-storage-and-disposal.

[41] See more broadly Fogleman (2023), pp. 208–212.

[42] 40 Code of Federal Regulations § 264.117(a)(1).

[43] Ibid §264.143(d) or § 265.143(c), (d).

estimated amount that would be paid to a third party to carry out the activities specified in the permit for the TSDF or HWMU.

The owner or operator of TSDFs must have financial security for "bodily injury and property damage to third parties caused by sudden accidental occurrences" that are induced by operations at the facility or a group of facilities, which constitute environmental liabilities requirement. Examples of sudden accidental occurrences include releases of hazardous waste caused by a fire or explosion—that is abrupt releases rather than continuous releases. Land TSDFs must also have financial security for third-party bodily injury and property damage caused by a facility's or a group of facilities' "nonsudden accidental occurrence". Examples of nonsudden accidental occurrences include a leak of liquid waste from a landfill or a surface impoundment that pollutes groundwater.

The following financial security instruments are acceptable: a financial test or self-insurance; a financial guarantee; an irrevocable letter of credit; an insurance policy; a surety bond; a trust fund[44]; and a combination of the above.[45] The minimum level of financial security required for third-party bodily injury and property damage from a sudden and accidental occurrence is $1,000,000 (EUR 992,335) for each occurrence, with an aggregate annual limit of $2,000,000 (EUR1,984,670). The minimum level of financial security required for third-party bodily injury and property damage from a nonsudden and accidental occurrence is $3,000,000 (EUR 2,977,005), with an aggregate annual limit of $6,000,000 (EUR 5,953,500). The requirements for sudden and nonsudden and accidental occurrences may be combined with a minimum level of $4,000,000 (EUR 3,969,000) for each occurrence with an aggregate annual limit of $8,000,000 (EUR 7,938,000).

States establish financial security, environmental liability and environmental responsibility requirements for solid waste treatment, transfer and disposal facilities, including landfills. The types of instruments and mechanisms are usually the same as for the TSDF.

4 Financial Security as a Personal Security

The term "personal security" is not understood in the same way in European countries. It is a broad counterpart to the term "proprietary security". Personal security encompasses all security rights in which a person (whether a natural person or a legal entity) is liable with all of their assets in order to secure an obligation of another person, the principal debtor. In contrast, proprietary security (which is often, but not necessarily, provided by the debtor of the secured claim) exposes the

---

[44] Trust funds and standby trust funds must be fully funded. Unlike trust funds and standby trust funds for environmental responsibility requirements, funds for them may not be gradually accumulated.

[45] 40 Code of Federal Regulations § 264.147.

secured creditor to a right for preferential satisfaction with respect to the specific encumbered assets.

There are two main types of personal security: dependent and independent. The former is the older of the two, with its roots in Roman law (fideiussio). In some legal orders, the institution of fideiussio has been retained.[46] In classical law, after its adoption by the *ius commune Fideiussio* became the basis of modern European surety law. Both Roman law and *the ius* commune had forms of personal security that were similar to suretyship, such as *mandatum qualificatum*, as well as special forms of suretyship, such as *promissio indemnitatis* or *fideiussio fideiussoris* (surety reimbursement). A guarantee is also included in such transactions. All these transactions were covered by the umbrella term *intercessio*: substitution of someone's debt. A common historical tradition has led to a remarkable similarity in European surety law. This is also true for English personal security law, whose "contract of guarantee" is understood as the equivalent of suretyship. It was influenced by Roman law, partly directly and partly through merchant law (*lex mercatoria*).[47]

Over centuries of practical experience, national rules have been established, although there is some variation between member states. In contrast, the independent personal security is a modern phenomenon. In some countries, it was not recognised until the late twentieth century, and it was only exceptionally sanctioned by legislators. The terms "dependent" and "independent" personal security are not derived from any national legal system. It was adopted in Principles, Definitions and Model Rules of European Private Law Draft Common Frame of Reference (DCFR), where the issue of "personal security" was discussed in Book IV Part. G.[48] The terms "dependent" and "independent" are used because they express the salient features of the two types. Personal security may either be dependent upon major aspects of the secured claim or it may be independent of any possibly underlying claim.

The basic institution is defined as suretyship or guarantee. However, none of these terms are firmly rooted or universally accepted. Consequently, the Study Group on a European Civil Code and the Research Group on the Existing EC Private Law (Acquis Group) have decided to coin a new functional and descriptive term "dependent personal security". In the vast majority of cases, a security provider

---

[46] The Romanian Civil Code defines fideiussio in art. 773 as: "the legal operation whereby one or more settlers transfer rights in rem, debt, securities or other property rights or a combination of such rights, current or future, to one or more fiduciaries performing the same with a specific purpose, for the benefit of one or more beneficiaries. These rights make up an autonomous assigned patrimony distinct from other rights and obligations of the fiduciaries 'properties". The *fiducia cum creditore* was to guarantee the fulfilment of an obligation, meaning that the debtor of the obligation transferred the creditor's asset, who in its turn, would commit to return the relevant asset as soon as the debtor would have fulfilled undertaken obligation - Daniel Moreanu, Fiducia si trust-ul, Editura, Bucuresti 2017, p. 53.

[47] Sonja Meier, Suretyship, Ius Commune <https://max-eup2012.mpipriv.de/index.php/Roman_Law>, Max-Eup 2012.

[48] Principles Definitions and Model Rules of European Private Law Draft Common Frame of Reference (DCFR) part. G.

promises to make a payment. The security provider may also offer to provide other services, such as the providing marketable securities or other goods. However, this form of security will not constitute a financial security, which is the focus of this study.

The secured obligation may take any form. In the majority of cases, it will be a monetary obligation. It may also be covering the costs of an action imposed by a decision of an administrative authority. All secured obligations may arise at the time of acceptance of the security obligation or in the future. For instance, a claim for damages in case of non-performance may be made by the waste holder. The secured obligation may be conditional. The person establishing a personal or property security interest may wish to be certain that they will be able to make a recourse claim against another person in the event of a claim under the security (i.e. holder of waste). There is no contraindication to securing such a conditional obligation of the security provider. Indeed, this type of security is frequently used in commercial practice and is also a feature of an insurance guarantee (more on this below).

Professional security providers, such as banks or insurance companies, typically charge a commission (premium) for the issue of dependent personal security. Consequently, such security is typically provided within a bilateral agreement, creating an obligation at least for the security provider. The debtor of the secured obligation (here the waste holder) is usually involved indirectly in two ways. In the relationship with the creditor (here, the administrative authority issuing the decision authorising the management of potentially hazardous waste), the debtor (waste holder) is required to involve the provider of the personal security, which must meet certain minimum conditions set by the creditor. These conditions are set out in an administrative decision. On the other hand, the debtor is obliged to request the security provider to grant a security interest in favour of a creditor meeting the requisite conditions. This results in the creation of a tripartite relationship. However, the content and purposes of each of the three sides of this triangle are distinct. Furthermore, the objectives of each of the three sides of this triangle differ (characterised by the guarantee). The two sides can be classified as types of bilateral contract. The first is a credit relationship between the creditor and the debtor, which is usually accompanied by a security agreement. The second is an assignment or service agreement between the debtor and the security provider. There is still a third side between the creditor and the security provider, which is the contractual dependent personal security, for example, a guarantee. In the present case, it is unlikely that all sides of the triangle will be bound by contracts, as the credit relationship between creditor and debtor is of an administrative-legal nature. Therefore, it is probable that a security requirement will arise from the content of the administrative-legal dilemma.

However, including the insurance activities in personal security is questionable. Paragraph 2 of IV.G.-1:102 CDFR explicitly excludes insurance contracts from the scope of the Principles. However, as the context indicates, liability insurance can be considered a type of personal security in a functional sense. The rationale for excluding this type of insurance from the personal security regulation is the general structure of insurance contracts, of which these contracts are only a part, and the specific European rules (principles of European insurance contract law) that are supposed to regulate them. Functionally, guarantee insurance is even more closely related to personal security than other types of insurance, since it is taken out by the debtor, usually at the request of and for the benefit of the creditor. This is acknowledged by the drafters of the DCFR, who allow to apply personal security provisions to an insurance guarantee, provided that the insurer has issued a document containing personal security in favour of the creditor (paragraph 2 of IV.G.-1:102 CDFR in fine).

5 Insurance Instruments Vs. Other Types of Financial Securities

The EU legislator has shown a liberal approach in regulating insurance instruments in waste management. It allows for the choice of collateral—whether by the entity applying for a specific waste permit or by the authority. The directives cited above are not uniform on these issues. However, it can be assumed that the authority issuing the permit has the decisive voice on the issue of financial security. It should be taken into account that in all cases the financial security is required for the activity of the given entity: a landfill manager, a mining plant or an electronic equipment producer, who we refer to collectively as the waste holder for the purposes of this study. What we are dealing with is a compulsory financial security of for a specific entrepreneur, which, however, cannot be treated as compulsory (or even mandatory) insurance.. The compulsion to insure is combined with the statutory obligation to take out an insurance contract. According to PEICL, "Compulsory insurance" means an insurance which is taken out in pursuance of an obligation to insure, imposed by laws or regulations (Article 1.202.10). In the cases in question, we are dealing with the imposition of financial security involving instruments of a different legal nature. We could speak of an insurance obligation only if, as part of the implementation, a Member State chose insurance as financial security and obliged the waste holder to purchase insurance cover on the basis of an insurance contract or insurance guarantee.

There is a kind of competition between different financial instruments as instruments for securing claims of public entities. The EU legislator limits itself to imposing "financial security or any other equivalent" (Landfill Directive), "financial guarantee or equivalent" (Extractive Waste Directive), "financial guarantee or equivalent insurance" (Shipments of Waste Regulation) and, most specifically, "the form of participation by the producer in appropriate schemes for the financing of the management of WEEE, a recycling insurance or a blocked bank account" (WEEE Directive). As we can see, there is a lack of uniformity in the formulation of the safeguards imposed by the EU legislator. The question arises as to whether the differences are justified by the specificity of waste management as regulated in the individual directives, or whether they indicate a lack of terminological precision on the part of the EU legislator. Such a general wording is consistent with the spirit of harmonisation and allows the Member State to adapt the requirement to the level of development of the national financial market. National legislation, therefore, usually indicates a few specific financial securities, from which the security is chosen in a particular case.

According to V. Fogleman: insurance is generally not a suitable financial security instrument for known environmental responsibilities, because insurance provides cover for fortuities, not certainties.[49] Applicable financial security instruments therefore tend to be bonds, bank guarantees, trust accounts and other such instruments. As part of the contractual agreement between the business and the authority, insurance may be applied in addition to the types of financial securities above in order to cover fortuities, such as time of landfill closure or a surface mine restoration. The duration of such necessary actions can be assessed only with some probability. Equating the concept of insurance with contract insurance is noteworthy. While contract insurance is the basic and most popular insurance activity, it is not the only one, and a second insurance activity such as an insurance guarantee should also be covered by the broad concept of insurance (more on the next chapter)). Insurance is widely recognised as an economic and legal category. The combination of economic and legal aspects is evident in the view of insurance as a risk management instrument.

Insurance (an insurance contract in particular) is often used to provide financial security. Insurance instruments (insurance contract and insurance guarantee) provide a comprehensive solution for an entrepreneur or public entity providing financial support in the event of disruption to their operations. Eliminating disruptions to operations or tasks caused by the realisation of risks threatening an entity is the basic function of insurance, which is considered to be the compensatory function. This affects the distribution of insurance and the extent of cover provided (as discussed further in Chapter V). Hence, financial security in the form of an insurance contract may often be the most natural and cheapest way for the waste holder to meet the financial security requirement.. This may be seen differently by the authority whose claims are affected by the security.

For example, in Poland, in accordance with the provisions of the Waste Act,[50]which is an implementation of the Landfill Directive, the waste management entity, in order to undertake and carry out its activities, is obliged to present a financial security in the form of: (1) bank deposit, (2) bank guarantee, (3) insurance guarantee, (4) insurance policy. The security in the form of a bank guarantee, an insurance guarantee or an insurance policy shall be submitted to the authority approving the instructions for operating the landfill site. The purpose of such action is to secure the claims of the State Treasury or local government entities acting through their respective competent administrative authorities (provinde marshal or Regional Directors for Environmental Protection) for the occurrence of negative effects and damage on the environment in connection with landfill operation

[49] Fogleman (2023), p. 79.

[50] Act of 14 December 2012 on waste (Polish Journal of Laws of 2013, item 21).

(damage to protected species, protected habitats, waters, soil). In accordance with Article 125 of the Waste Act, the bank guarantee, insurance guarantee or insurance policy should state that, in case of negative effects on the environment or environmental damage, the bank or insurer will settle the obligations if the competent authority (province marshal) decides to use the funds from the security of claims for the remediation of these effects, insofar as these actions have not been performed by the landfill manager at his own expense (similarly, Article 48a(17) of the Waste Act). The requirement of such a declaration, as well as its content, may constitute a significant factor hindering the use of insurance as the required contract security. One has to agree with the view that limiting the obligation to trigger security to situations where the landfill manager has failed to remedy adverse environmental effects or environmental damage at his own expense could be hardly acceptable under insurance law. This is if we assume that the purpose of the security is to satisfy claims against the security holder, i.e. to discharge the obligation of personal performance. This is the intention behind the conclusion of an third party insurance contract, including such kind of environmental insurance. The policyholder gets insurance protection in return for a relatively low premium in relation to the costs he would have to bear if the covered event occurred. In this way, the policyholder protects his property interests by transferring part of his financial consequence of its responsibility to another entity—the insurer.[51] This immanent feature of insurance can be a barrier to choosing this form of security. The security regulated by the Waste Act does not lead to a transfer of the financial burden resulting from the responsibility of the landfill manager, in case of negative effects on the environment or environmental damage. There is a significant narrowing of the scope of the insurer's liability to cover expenses for remediation of the negative effects on the environment and environmental damage incurred by the public entity (here the province marshal), when the insured does not incur such costs.

Difficulties in the use of insurance are indicated by the specific case of Zakład Utylizacji Odpadów Sp z o.o., which applied for an integrated permit for a thermal waste conversion facility issued by the Marshall of the Wielkopolskie Province as the competent authority in this matter. In accordance with Article 48a(1) to (4) of the Waste Act, it was obliged to obtain a permit for waste processing as a waste holder that is not the operator of a landfill to which the abovementioned Article 125 of the Waste Act applies. Obtaining the permit requires establishing a security for claims to cover the costs of substitutive performance of: a) a decision ordering the removal of waste from a place not intended for landfill or storage, b) the removal of waste, negative effects or damage to the environment caused in the event of permit withdrawal, or c) the need to remove waste or residues after a firefighting action or the removal of negative effects or damage to the environment. The operator of the installation—Zakład Utylizacji Odpadów Sp z o.o., declared tthe claims security in the form of an insurance policy covering PLN 1,500,000 (one million five hundred thousand zlotys). In accordance with Article 48a(7) of the Waste Act, the Marshal of

[51] Orzechowska (2021a), p. 51.

the Wielkopolskie Province specified the abovementioned form and amount of the claims security in his decision. According to Article 48a(10) of the Waste Act, Zakład Utylizacji Odpadów presented the original insurance policy to the authority. The authority found that the submitted policy did not meet the requirements set out in the Waste Act, in particular with regard to the insurer's statement concerning the payment of obligations to the competent enforcement authority, and obliged the operator to re-submit a document confirming establishing security of claims, meeting the condition referred to in Article 48a(5) of the Waste Act.[52] In response to the above, Zakład Utylizacji Odpadów changed the form of the claim security—from an insurance policy to a bank guarantee. The Marshal of the Wielkopolskie Province, by way of a decision, redefined the abovementioned form (bank guarantee) and the amount of the claim security (PLN 1,500,000).[53]

Failure to include the statutory statement in the insurance policy may happen due to at least two reasons: (1) the incorrect perception of the insurance policy as a legal transaction (2) the essence of the insurer's benefit which amounts to insurance protection in relation to the assumed risk of an uncertain event.[54] The first reason is characteristic of continental law, where the insurance policy is only a document confirming the conclusion of an insurance contract.[55] It does not constitute a source of obligation and the statements contained therein only confirm the content of the contract concluded by implication. Unfortunately, the Polish Waste Act explicitly refers to the insurance policy as financial security which loses sight of its nature. This results in the authority focusing on the content of the policy. The second reason seems to be of key importance in examining the adequacy of the insurance contract as a financial security for claims of administrative authorities covering the costs of activities related to the removal of negative changes in the environment. It results from an administrative decision issued on the basis of specific provisions concerning a particular waste holder (landfill operator, producer of waste shipped abroad). The purpose of the security is to provide security for the payment of obligations to the enforcement authority of the waste holder.

Such assurance requires a specific definition of insured event—a concept crucial to the formation of the insurance relationship. According to the doctrine, an insurance accident is the materialisation of an insurance risk, independent of the will of

[52] The wording of Article 48 a section 5 reads: 'The bank guarantee, insurance guarantee or insurance policy shall state that at any time, until a final decision on the return of the bank guarantee, insurance guarantee or insurance policy referred to in paragraph 18 is issued, in the event of adverse effects on the environment or environmental damage within the meaning of the Act of 13 April 2007 on prevention of damage to the environment and its remediation, arising as a result of the entity's failure to comply with the obligations set out in this Act, including the obligations arising from its waste collection permit or waste processing permit, or the need to remove waste from a place not intended for its storage or landfill, the bank or insurance company shall pay the obligations to the authority enforcing these obligations.'

[53] Decision of the Marshal of the Wielkopolskie Voivodeship of 30.11.2020, DSR-II-2.7222.34.2019 https://bip.umww.pl/artykuly/2826939/pliki/20210316115713_7222.34.pdf.

[54] Instead of many Maśniak (2022), p. 1225.

[55] Widely D. Fuchs (2009), pp. 19—26.

the policyholder (insured), which is characterised by uncertainty.[56] While defining "insured event", PEICL limits itself to "materialisation of the risk specified in the insurance contract" (Art. 1.201(2)). An appropriate definition of an insurance event provided by the insurer in the insurance terms and conditions may be a solution. This is possible in property insurance (or indemnity insurance, adopting the classification provided in PEICL) other than liability insurance—which is dependent on the liability of the insured due to its accessory nature. For example, the Polish Civil Code stipulates that in liability insurance "the insurer undertakes to pay compensation, specified in the contract, for damage caused to third parties to whom the insurer or the insured is liable" (Article 822 of the Polish Civil Code). According to the PEICL, "Liability insurance" means insurance where the risk means the exposure of the insured to legal liability towards the victim" (Article 1.201.5) and "the insured event shall be the fact giving rise to the insured's liability" (Article 14.107.1). Assuming that issuing a final decision of a competent enforcement authority on the allocation of funds from the claims security established to cover the costs of substitute performance during the insurance period will constitute the insurance event does not negate the attribute of uncertainty—immanent to an insurance accident.[57] Such a definition solves the problem raised in the doctrine about adjusting the scope of insurance protection to the extent expected by the legislator—the security should require the release of funds, regardless of whether there is a direct risk of damage to the environment or the damage to the environment is done.[58]

The specificity of the financial security established to "ensure that all obligations flowing from the permit have been fulfilled" (recital 28 of the preamble to the Landfill Directive) also affects the temporal scope of the protection. It is in the interest of the environmental authority, and arguably in the context of the Directive, to assume that the security covers all obligations owed to the waste manager, regardless of when they arise. Such a solution is not acceptable to insurers. Hence, the clauses (triggers) adopted on the insurance market stipulating that the insurance protection covers accidents resulting from failures committed by the insured up to 3 years preceding the beginning of the insurance period indicated in the insurance contract.[59]

Such insurance, suitably "tailored" to the needs imposed by EU law, can hardly be regarded as third party insurance. As insurance covers preventive and remedial costs related to waste management, it should be classified under insurance group 16

[56] The definition of a fortuitous event adopted in the Polish Insurance and Reinsurance Act of 11 September 2015, Polish Journal of Laws of 2015 No 1844 (Article 3(1)(57)) reads "fortuitous event - a future and uncertain event, independent of the will of the policyholder or the insured, the occurrence of which causes damage to personal property or property or an increase in property needs on the part of the policyholder or another person covered by the insurance protection".

[57] Such a solution is already used in the insurance market, but is unfortunately a rarity—Environmental, Protect, General, Terms and Conditions of Indemnity Insurance for Environmental Damages—the General Terms and Conditions of Colonnade Insurance S.A.

[58] Orzechowska (2021b), pp. 79–82.

[59] Environmental Protection - the General Terms and Conditions of Colonnade Insurance S.A.

(insurance of various financial risks). This classification is all the more justified when we bear in mind that they represent an alternative to an insurance guarantee—an insurance activity covering also financial risk.

A comparison of the national solutions which are an expression of the implementation of the EU financial security rules shows the absence of environmental insurance as the sole mean of financial security for measures such as landfill or other waste facility closure or aftercare. Insurance may be used to provide cover for the risk of, say, landfill or waste facility closure whose costs exceed the estimated costs, the operator being required to close the landfill or waste facility before the planned date for doing so, or environmental damage from incidents during closure or aftercare. Other financial security instruments, such as guarantees, security deposits or bonds, however, are required to cover the estimated costs of closure and aftercare. This is because the insurance protection covers fortuities, but not certainties. According to principle of indemnity, indemnity is a guarantee to restore the insured to the position he or she was in before the *uncertain* incident that caused a loss for the insured. However, the statement that "insurance may be part of the financial security for responsibilities but only to the extent that liabilities may arise from them" does not see the opportunity offered by financial risk insurance and focuses on third party insurance (liability insurance).[60]

Unfortunately, today in the twenty-first century, creditors (competent authorities) deciding in the scope of its competence) on the form of financial security often choose a security deposit. For administrative bodies, the simplest and surest way to secure their claims is to deposit the amount of money used as financial security. A security deposit is money held in a bank account or with other financial institution that requires a transfer from one party (holder of waste) to another (bank or another financial institution). Such a deposit means that the entrepreneur (waste holder) is unable to use the entire secured amount for the entire period of their business operation. From the waste holder perspective, a security deposit is the least advantageous form of financial security.

Although the foregoing analysis identifies several structural and doctrinal obstacles that currently constrain the effectiveness of insurance as a form of financial security for environmental risks, these limitations cannot be regarded as sufficient grounds for excluding insurance from the catalogue of permissible instruments. Rather, they demonstrate that the present difficulties arise not from any inherent incapacity of insurance to perform a security function, but from a lack of congruence between the legal nature of insurance protection and the manner in which environmental legislation conceptualises financial security. The issues outlined above—such as the tension between indemnification for fortuitous events and statutory requirements to ensure the availability of funds for foreseeable environmental obligations, the formulation of insurer responsibilities in terms that are incompatible with the doctrinal framework of insurance contracts, and the statutory narrowing of insurance coverage to circumstances in which the waste holder bears no

[60] Fogleman (2020), p. 48.

costs—constitute manifestations of regulatory incoherence rather than evidence of the inadequacy of insurance as such. These tensions indicate the need to reconsider and recalibrate the normative framework governing insurance-based financial security so that the instrument may be adapted to the specific characteristics of environmental obligations without undermining the foundational principles of insurance law. The objective is therefore not to maintain insurance despite its deficiencies, but to acknowledge its legal and functional advantages—particularly its capacity to allocate risk, mobilise private capital and mitigate liquidity burdens on waste holders—and to examine how the regulatory framework might be refined to ensure that insurance can operate as a coherent and legally sound mechanism of financial security.

References

Betlem G (1995) It's no use crying over spilt chemicals. Maastricht J Eur Comp Law 2(3):294

Bocken H (2009) Alternative financial guarantees for environmental liabilities under the ELD. Eur Energy Environ Law Rev 18(3):146–151

Church TW, Nakamura RT (1994) Beyond superfund: hazardous waste cleanup in Europe and the United States. Georgetown Int Environ Law Rev 7:41–42

Dent GW (1991) Limited liability in environmental law. Wake Forest Law Rev 26(1):151–182

Fogleman V (2015) Landowners' liability for remediating contaminated land in the EU: EU or national law? Part II: national law. Environ Liabil 23(2):42–61

Fogleman V (2020) Improving financial security in the context of the environmental liability directive. Publications Office of the European Union

Fogleman V (2023) Environmental liabilities and insurance law in the European Union. In: Maśniak D, Malinowska K (eds) Managing environmental risk through insurance. Springer

Fuchs D (2009) Charakter prawny polisy ubezpieczeniowej w prawie polskim a przedmiotowy zakres zastosowania Konwencji Wiedeńskiej o umowach międzynarodowej sprzedaży towarów z 1980 r. Przyczynek do wykładni norm międzynarodowego prawa handlowego. Rozprawy Ubezpieczeniowe 1(6)

Hosseinpour M, Osanloo M, Azimi Y (2022) Evaluation of positive and negative impacts of mining on sustainable development by a semi-quantitative method. J Clean Prod 366:Article 132955

Ireland P (2010) Limited liability, shareholder rights and the problem of corporate irresponsibility. Cambridge J Econ 34(5):845–847

Maśniak D (2016) Road accident victim transboundary protection system. Gdansk

Maśniak D (2022) Umowa ubezpieczenia. In: Małgorzata Balwicka-Szczyrba, A (ed) Kodeks cywilny. Komentarz. Sylwestrzak, Warsaw

Maunumäki A (2020) Mining, remediation, and financial guarantees the Swedish implementation of the Extractive Waste Directive 2006/21. Uppsala Universitet

Ociepa-Kicińska E (2023) Socio-economic challenges of removing and disposing of illegal hazardous waste dumps: poland case study. Eur Res Stud J XXVI(3):570–583

Orzechowska R (2021a) Odpowiedzialność podmiotu korzystającego ze środowiska – narzędzia mitygacji finansowych konsekwencji odpowiedzialności za szkodę w środowisku za pomocą ubezpieczeń, Prawo Asekuracyjne No. 1/2021

Orzechowska R (2021b) Environmental liability of the operator – financial tools to mitigate the consequences of environmental liability with insurance. In: Malinowska K, Maśniak D, Tarasiuk A (eds) Environmental risk and insurance. Publishing House of the University of Gdańsk

Owen GR, Kemp D, Lèbre É, Svobodova K, Pérez Murillo G (2020) Catastrophic tailings damures and disaster risk disclosure. Int J Disaster Risk Reduction, tom 42
Twum E (2013) Legislative regulation and financial institutions in environmental assurance in developing countries: Case study of mining in Ghana. Afr J Polit Sci Int Relat 7:200–208
Vaverková MD, Maxianová A, Winkler J, Adamcová D, Podlasek A (2019) Environmental consequences and the role of illegal waste dumps and their impact on land degradation. Land Use Policy 89

Waste Insurance Guarantee

1 Introduction

The present chapter is devoted to an in-depth examination of the insurance guarantee and its relevance as a legal and economic instrument for securing risks arising in waste management. The absence of a uniform regulatory framework governing insurance guarantees calls for a more detailed doctrinal analysis of their legal nature, taking into account different legal cultures and the historical evolution of guarantee instruments. This requires determining how the insurance guarantee should be positioned within contract law and identifying whether it constitutes a distinct type of guarantee contract. Such an inquiry naturally leads to an exploration of the similarities and differences between guarantee insurance and other guarantee-based instruments.

In this context, a further question concerns the structural dimension of the insurance guarantee, including whether it should be conceptualised as a tripartite legal relationship and, if so, how this differs from tripartite constructions such as insurance in favour of a third party. Addressing the characteristics that define the insurance guarantee necessitates a systematic comparison with institutions performing analogous security functions, notably suretyship, security deposits, bank guarantees and insurance contracts. Each of these instruments offers a different balance of legal protection, economic burden and functional suitability.

Given the overarching aim of the dissertation, it is essential to identify which differences between these institutions are decisive when they are used by waste holders as financial security mechanisms required by environmental authorities. Only such an integrated analysis makes it possible to determine the functional value of the insurance guarantee in waste management and to evaluate whether, and under what conditions, it may constitute an effective and economically justified alternative to other forms of financial security.

D. Maśniak, *The Legal Framework for the Use of Insurance in Ecological Waste Management*, AIDA Europe Research Series on Insurance Law and Regulation 17, https://doi.org/10.1007/978-3-032-26550-0_5

2 Insurance Guarantee as an Insurance Activity

Insurance is involved when an obligation to pay in the event of certain events is assumed in return for payment. The assumed risk is shared among a number of persons at risk, and the assumption itself is based on a calculation based on the law of large numbers.[1] The criterion of the community of risks (German: *Gefahrengemeinschaft*) is an organisational feature of insurance business, which boils down to the performance of insurance activities. Building the community of risk allows to apply the law of large numbers and determine an appropriate premium for risk bearing. In the case of both insurance contract and guarantee insurance provided as security related to waste management, building a community of risk can be difficult due to the specificity of non-standard activities, which is necessary from the point of view of qualifying these activities as insurance activities.[2]

The EU legislator classified insurance risks by groups in the annex to the Solvency II Directive.[3] It is of vital importance because of the principle of insurance licensing that requires insurers to obtain authorisation to conduct insurance business in certain classes. An analysis of the EU classification does not directly identify the risk corresponding to the risk covered by insurance guarantees. The way in which the Directive and its Annex have been implemented in some Member States indicates group 15 (Suretyshift). The risks included in group 15 are sometimes understood as a guarantee, as evidenced by Member States legislation implementing the above-mentioned directive (see Poland). However, one should be careful when equating insurance risks that define the scope of insurance activity of public nature with civil law transactions that are part of this insurance activity.

The Polish Act on Insurance and Reinsurance Activity[4] (implementing the Solvency II Directive) empowers insurers to conclude insurance contracts and guarantee contracts.[5] It clearly limits the insurer's options in terms of the ways to provide insurance cover. Other European legislatures do not introduce an additional category of insurance activities (see Germany), focusing on regulations concerning the insurance contract. Due to the fact that the insurance guarantee is a non-regulated contract, the lack of regulations devoted to it does not make it inadmissible in such countries.

[1] Court Decision BVerwG of 12.5.1992 r., 1 A 126/89, NJW 1992, p. 2978; similarly Court Decision BVerwG of 29.9.1992 r., 1 A 26/91, VersR 1992, p. 1217 – cit. per. Förster (2010), [The Fusion of Accessory Suretyship and Independent Guarantee. A New Systematization from the Perspective of Comparative Law.] p. 135.

[2] Förster (2010), p. 137.

[3] Directive 2009/138/EC of the European Parliament and of the Council of 25 November 2009 on the taking-up and pursuit of the business of Insurance and Reinsurance (Solvency II) (recast) (Text with EEA relevance) OJ L 335, 17.12.2009, pp. 1–155.

[4] Act of 11 September 2015 on insurance and reinsurance activity, Polish Journal of Laws of 2015, item 1844.

[5] It follows from Article 7 Section 7 point 1 of the Act on insurance and reinsurance activity—cf. judgement of the Regional Court in Warsaw of 13 June 2017, XXVI GC 291/13.

Assuming that the EU legislator understands suretyship (group 15) as a guarantee, the Solvency II Directive in Article 13(27)(b) classifies guarantees as so-called large risks, "where the policy holder is engaged professionally in an industrial or commercial activity or in one of the liberal professions and the risks relate to such activity". It results in a possibility to subject such a guarantee contract to the law chosen by the parties on the basis of Article 7(2) of Regulation (EC) No 593/2008 of the European Parliament and of the Council of 17.06.2008 on the law applicable to contractual obligations (Rome I), as well as a possibility to conclude a jurisdiction agreement pursuant to Article 16(5) of Regulation (EU) No 1215/2012 of the European Parliament and of the Council of 12 December 2012 on jurisdiction and the recognition and enforcement of judgments in civil and commercial matters. The distinction of large risks in EU law is intended to identify those insurance risks that are subject to less stringent conditions than other insurance risks, known as mass risks.

A different situation arises where insurance contracts are relied upon as a mechanism for protecting against waste risks. Such insurance contracts may relate to risks classified—in accordance with Annex I to the Solvency II Directive—under Class 13 (General Liability) or Class 16 (Miscellaneous Financial Loss), as discussed in greater detail in Chapter V. In both cases, Article 13(27)(c) of the Solvency II Directive applies. This provision stipulates that such risks qualify as large risks," insofar as the policyholder exceeds the limits of at least two of the following criteria: (i) a balance sheet total of EUR 6.2 million; (ii) a net turnover, within the meaning of Fourth Council Directive 78/660/EEC of 25 July 1978 based on Article 54(3) (g) of the Treaty on the annual accounts of certain types of companies, of EUR 12.8 million; (iii) an average number of 250 employees during the financial year".

3 Insurance Guarantee: Legal Nature

3.1 Guarantee Contract in Different Legal Cultures

Using the term guarantee in a number of contexts creates an important problem in assessing the legal nature of an insurance guarantee. Guarantee liability is treated as a separate indemnity regime. A representative example of that is the liability of the insurer[6] under both the insurance contract and the guarantee contract (more on the relationship between insurance contract and guarantee insurance below). In contract law, there are guarantee relationships also named warranties, generally referring to a quality guarantee of goods or services provided by its producer.[7] The concept of

[6] Kaliński (2008), p. 48 et seq.

[7] Common law provides for the institution of express (contractual) warranties as the equivalent of warranty-type assurances, in particular concerning the characteristics of a sold thing—Grossman (1981), p. 461 et seq.

warranty fits into the framework of contract law as it constitutes an assumption of liability if a thing does not have characteristics specified in the contract.[8] Guaranty relates to the future and is intended to protect the creditor from damage incurred as a result of a third party's failure to satisfy its obligations. Warranty, on the other hand, refers to the present or the past and is intended to protect the entitled person from damage if things do not turn out as the debtor has reassured. It is also argued that the warranty is already broken when it is granted if things are different than what was assured.[9]

Both guarantee (insurance and banking), insurance contract and surety can be classified as broadly understood guarantee contracts. The construction of the guarantee contract as a separate legal institution did not develop until the nineteenth century.[10] In this respect, there is an important difference in regard to, for example, surety, which was a relatively well-defined institution already in the ancient laws.[11] The literature emphasises that the guarantee is a product of modern legal thought and that the etymology of the term originates from the Germanic languages.[12] German literature points out that the term originates from the Old High German *wëren*, from where it passed into French to take the form *garantir*, and then returned in this altered form to German in the seventeenth century as *gewähren* or *gewährleisten* (nowadays, the last wording appears mainly in the context of liability for defects or lack of properties).[13]

French legal culture generally adopted a broad concept of a collateral action (French: *garantie*) which did not imply any particular legal institution, but rather referred to the broad concept of security (French: *sûreté*).[14] The term *garantie* functions as a broad concept, whereby different legal constructs can be understood under this one term—depending on the context. The term *garantie* does not refer to a specific legal construct and is not a technical term of legal or juridical language, but rather an umbrella term covering various types of security constructs.[15] This concept was not limited to personal securities, but also included collateral security.[16] Towards te end of the twentieth century, the confidence in international markets decreased due to the oil crisis in the 1970s. There is a growing interest in such safeguards, the effectiveness of which does not depend on the legal formation of the underlying (covered) relationships, which may be subject to the legal orders of different states. As a results, the concepts of an autonomous guarantee and a first demand guarantee

[8] Rabel (1950), p. 277.

[9] Garner (2019).

[10] Cf. Łętowska (1970), pp. 18 and 22.

[11] Förster (2010), p. 3.

[12] 5; Förster (2010), p. 39; Radin (1929), p. 605.

[13] T. Bär, Zum Rechtsbegriff der Garantie, insbesondere im Bankgeschäft, Dissertation der Rechts- und staatswissenschaftlichen Fakultät der Universität Zürich zur Erlangung der Würde eines Doktors beider Rechte, Winterthur 1963, p. 4 after Jastrzębski (2021), chapter 2 § 3.

[14] Kleiner (1979), pp. 124 and 126.

[15] Netter (2010), cf. Förster (2010), p. 60.

[16] As to a broad understanding of the concept of garantie see also Netter (2010), pp. 24–26.

emerged as independent legal constructs.[17] Internationalisation (globalisation) is recognised in the literature as a driver of this development.[18] Eventually, the needs of international trade led first the doctrine and then the legislature to develop the concept of an autonomous guarantee as a legal construct. It was expressed in Article 2321 of the French Civil Code introduced in 2006.[19] Research presented in more recent literature aimed at defining the essence of the guarantee contract (*garantie indemnitaire*) as a specific legal construct rather than an umbrella term. It has led to proposing a core of this institution in the form of an obligation to cover risks (*obligation de couverture*), which is close to an insurance approach.[20] The proposed concept of *obligation de couverture* and perceiving *couverture* as a contractual obligation is a kind of structural convergence of collateral actions (e.g. suretyship), guarantee contracts (e.g. a third party service agreement, but also a guarantee of the warrants against defects of a subject of sale) and insurance. What all these contracts have in common is the presence of a *couverture de risque* as a specific subject of contractual obligation.[21] The point is a performance by the guarantor for the guarantee beneficiary, by which the guarantor assumes the risks that would otherwise be borne by the beneficiary. Coverage of risks understood in this way constitutes the subject of an obligation—a contractual obligation which in turn may be manifested by partial acts or omissions designed to provide the beneficiary with the intended protection.[22] In the case of *garanties indemnitaires*, indemnity (French: *l'indemnisation*) is intended to be an act under the guarantee of risk coverage. The concept of an autonomous guarantee (French: *garantie autonome*) in French law has traditionally been constructed in opposition to suretyship and its accessoriness, which entails weaker collateral function, leading to a search for new forms of security.[23] A non-accessory unconditional guarantee payable on first demand is a model example of an autonomous guarantee under French law.[24]

The concept of contract of indemnity, known in the common law system, covered all cases where someone undertook to indemnify another person against harm in the broadest sense.[25] In this broad sense, the contract of indemnity covered, in addition to the security of claims, property insurance[49]. Further distinctions in this regard were associated with the English Statute of Frauds from the seventeenth century, which introduced formal requirements for certain types of acts, including contracts that were a source of liability for debt or actions of another person ("a

[17] Cf. Förster (2010), s. 60, 61.

[18] Pyziak-Szafnicka (1994), pp. 17–26.

[19] Förster (2010), p. 60.

[20] Cf. E. Netter (2010), p. 256.

[21] On the evolution of the construction of insurance and the developmental conditions of the regulation of this institution in French law, see (Netter 2010, pp. 197–207).

[22] Netter (2010), p. 253.

[23] Netter (2010), pp. 18–24.

[24] Netter (2010), p. 85.

[25] *B. Kleiner*, Bankgarantie, p. 128.

special promise to answer for the debt, default or miscarriages of another person").[26] The Statute of Frauds led to distinguishing constructions similar to suretyship, which in English and US law include guarantee (treated simplistically as an equivalent of surety) and suretyship (treated simplistically as an equivalent of cumulative assumption of debt). Collaterally, another construction was distinguished. In this construction, the guarantor assumes an independent obligation, unrelated to the debt of another person—that is esentially indemnity in its narrow sense. It is noted, however, that the Statute of Frauds does not use concepts such as guarantee, suretyship or indemnity. However, it refers to the assumption of liability for a debt or third party's failure to satisfy its obligations, so in theory the distinction between these institutions does not need to be conclusive from the point of view of the Statute of Frauds.[27] In the common law legal culture, there is virtually no problem of defining a guarantee contract and grasping its distinctiveness from other obligation agreements. It may be an expression of the pragmatic approach of the doctrine, which is oriented towards the resolution of specific legal problems rather than purely conceptual or terminological issues. However, the reason may also be different, related to another definition of the nature of the obligation and the liability associated with breach of obligation (non-performance—continental civil law) or breach of contract (breach of contract—common law). The essence of guarantee is that the promisor undertakes to indemnify the creditor against loss incurred in the course of his relationship with the debtor.[28] In judicial decisions, a juxtaposition of indemnity and guarantee as equivalent concepts is noticeable.[29] Under the guarantee, the guarantor is liable for performing the obligation by another person, and thus his liability is secondary to that of the principal debtor. There may be dependencies between the debtor's liability and the guarantor's liability relating for example to the extent of the liability (coextensive) or its duration (coterminous). English and US law do not make a sharp distinction between insurance and indemnity. Rather, it seems that insurance is treated as a special case of indemnity, which, in addition to the assumption of risk, is also characterised by its distribution and a number of other, less fundamental distinguishing features. A characteristic feature of the Anglo-American model is the distinction of surety-type guarantees (also found in other models) and the popularity of using indemnity as "non-professional insurance" for various risks

[26] "Contract to answer for requisite. The debt, default, or miscarriage of another person (a), and it being also a promise to be answerable for a debt of, or a default in, some duty by that other person towards the promisee (b)"—Biggs et al. (December 17, 2010), p. 562.

[27] Jastrzębski (2021), chapter 2 § 5 Legalis.

[28] Courtney (2014), p. 239. Similarly 38 American Jurisprudence 2d Guaranty § 11: "*a guaranty agreement is a species of an indemnity contract, in that a promisor agrees to be responsible for the performance of another even though the promisor does not have direct control over the performance of the principal obligation. However, while a guaranty contract is collateral and secondary to the principal contract, the promise in a contract of indemnity creates a primary liability*".

[29] Ruling of the California Court of Appeals (2nd district, division one) of 22 July 1969 on *Goodman v. Severin*, 79 Cal. Rptr., p. 555 et seq. and Ruling of the Superior Court of New Jersey (Appellate Division) of 29 July 2008 on *Feigenbaum v. Guaracini*, 952 A.2d, p. 511 et seq.

related to the activity to which the contract containing the indemnity clause relates.[30] The unwritten Anglo-Irish common law contains largely consistent rules. In the United States, the common law is summarized in the Restatement 3rd, Suretyship and Guaranty (1996)[31] which merges these two branches into one instrument.

In German-speaking legal culture, the guarantee contract has been contrasted with the established construct of suretyship through the use of the independence criteria of the guarantee and the accessory nature of the suretyship.[32] Current German law does not contain a general statutory definition of a guarantee contract1. In the course of the codification work on the BGB, in connection with the regulation of suretyship (§ 765 BGB), it was concluded that suretyship may be regulated as a special case of a guarantee contract, and there is no need for special norms for a guarantee contract.[33] It remains generally unregulated to this day, and its admissibility is beyond doubt and can be derived from the principle of freedom of contracts constructed on the basis of § 311 BGB and Article 2 Section 1 GG. In BGH jurisprudence, a guarantee contract is one by which someone undertakes to be liable for the occurrence of a certain result or to assume the risk of future damage.[34] The BGH judicial decisions identify the obligation to indemnify (cover damage) in the event that the expected result does not occur as a feature of a guarantee contract.[35] German doctrine has also formulated concepts based on the criterion of the creditor's interest and the desire to secure it. According to this approach, a guarantee contract is a non-reciprocal agreement that aims to secure a specific financial interest of the beneficiary in a way that the guarantor undertakes to compensate for the damage resulting from the failure to fulfil that interest. The lack of mutuality helps to distinguish such a guarantee contract from an insurance contract.[36] Within the idea that the essence of a guarantee contract is to secure a specific interest of the beneficiary, it is precisely the diversity of potential interests that makes it possible, within a broad understanding of a guarantee, to introduce its various forms. If it is in the interest of the beneficiary that a third party performs the contractual obligations (German: Leistung), we deal with a so-called performance guarantee (German: Leistungsgarantie). If, on the other hand, the beneficiary's interest concerns, for example, a certain properties of a given object (e.g. a thing), the guarantee securing this interest is a so-called property guarantee (German: Eigenschaftsgarantie).[37] The insurance guarantee under examination, in the light of this concept, constitutes an

[30] Jastrzębski (2021), chapter 2 § 2.

[31] Restatement of the law, third: suretyship and guaranty; as adopted and promulgated by the American Law Institute at Washington, D.C., May 19, 1995.

[32] Kleiner (1979), pp. 129–130.

[33] Förster (2010), pp. 51–52.

[34] BGH of 13 June 1996, IX ZR 172/95, NJW 1996, p. 2570, as well as the rulings cited by Förster (2010), p. 56, annotation 124.

[35] BGH of 12 February 1981, IVa ZR 103/80, NJW 1981, p. 2295: Ruling of BGH of 10 February 1999, VIII ZR 70/98, NJW 1999, p. 1543.

[36] Boetius (1966), p. 15 after Jastrzębski (2021), chapter 2 § 2.

[37] Boetius (1966), p. 2, 3 after Jastrzębski (2021), chapter 2 § 2 Legalis.

obligation performance guarantee. In each case, the guarantor's performance aims to remove the negative consequences for the beneficiary in case of failure to realise the secured interest: in the first case, the failure of the third party to perform the contractual obligations, and in the second case, the lack of certain properties of a given object (e.g. a thing). The usefulness of a broad view of the guarantee contract has been questioned in more recent German literature. It points out the low practical and cognitive value of such a broad view of the guarantee contract because of the variety of forms covered.[38] This concretisation was achieved, i.a. by excluding the so-called insurance-type guarantee (German: Versicherungsgarantie) from the concept of guarantee, which was proposed to be considered together with insurance.[39] The concept of an insurance-type guarantee (German: Versicherungsgarantie) covers the general formula of a letter of indemnity (or 'indemnification', German: Schadloshaltungsversprechen) that may involve any risk. The concept of an insurance-type guarantee refers to the idea that, by virtue of a guarantee contract, the risk of any event is assumed—with results in the obligation to compensate for damage resulting from its occurrence or non-occurrence.[40]

3.2 Insurance Guarantee v. Others Guarantee Contracts

The nature of guarantee insurance manifests itself where the traditional instrumentality of liability for breach of a pre-existing obligation proves inadequate, and the guarantor's liability is created by a contract, however, the compensation is the initial obligation, and not the consequence of breaching of another obligation by the debtor. The contractual assumption of risks by one person (the guarantor) that would otherwise be borne by another person (the guarantee beneficiary, the creditor under the guarantee) is part of the definition of a guarantee contract.[41] In this respect, there is therefore no difference between the insurance contract and other guarantee contracts.

In each case, there is an insurance protection against the consequences of events that would be borne by a creditor under general principles. Guarantee insurance is distinguished from other guarantee contracts by building a community of risks covered by the guarantee. The infrequency of the provision of cover will weigh against qualifying the contract as guarantee insurance. A feature of insurance is the assumption of mass and repetitive contracting.[42] In other guarantee contracts (except perhaps for a bank guarantee), the guarantor does not use statistical and actuarial methods to determine the insurance premium. The premium is not an equivalent for

[38] Förster (2010), p. 128.
[39] Förster (2010), p. 131.
[40] Förster (2010), p. 132.
[41] Förster (2010), p. 127.
[42] Jastrzębski (2018), pp. 4–15.

the risk assumed by the guarantor in such contracts. The difference between guarantee insurance and other guarantee contracts comes down to the *essentialium negotii* of insurance—the premium, as opposed to the absence of a strictly distinguishable consideration—e.g. in the form of a premium or commission—in other guarantee contracts. This difference should not be understood as if a guarantee contract other than an insurance contract is concluded solely in the interest of the guarantee beneficiary, or that the guarantor does not pursue its economic objectives by concluding it. Such a contract is often a part of a larger transaction and the guarantor's interest lies in the fact that, by entering into the guarantee contract, he leads to a larger transaction or obtains more favourable terms in other areas. Guarantee contract's aim is therefore not, at least in principle, to provide a free financial benefit to the beneficiary.[43] The fact that it is chargeable must, however, be viewed differently and more broadly than is the case with insurance. In particular, it is not based on the concept of a premium as a monetary value corresponding to a statistically determined probability of an insurer's obligation to pay. Moreover, such a construction of charge would not be possible if the risk pool inherent in insurance relationships is not created. The distinction between an insurance and a non-insurance guarantee contract requires considering the nature of the premium as the monetary equivalent of the statistically determined risk assumed by the insurer. By paying the premium, each policyholder participates in the risk covered by the risk pool. This is because the economic cost of this risk is distributed among all policyholders, who bear it somewhat upfront by agreeing to pay a premium The "mutual" characteristic attributed to insurance liability manifests this way.[44]

3.3 *Insurance Guarantee as Tripartite Relationship*

The insurance guarantee covers, in essence, three legal relationships that make up the guarantee relationship: 1. the so-called basic legal relationship between the debtor (obligor) and the creditor—beneficiary of the guarantee, 2. the relationship resulting from the contract linking the debtor (obligor) and the guarantor (guarantee application), and 3. guarantee contract between the creditor (beneficiary) and the guarantor—insurer (guarantee contract).[45] Mechanizm działania gwarancji ubezpieczeniowej można przedstawić na następującym schemacie: Ubezpieczyciel (A) udziela gwarancji na zlecenie osoby B. Osoba ta dokonała lub chce dokonać czynności prawnej (np. zawrzeć umowę sprzedaży) z osobą C (wierzycielem, beneficjentem gwarancji). There is a basic legal relationship between persons B and

[43] Jastrzębski (2021), chapter 4 § 4 Legalis.

[44] Cf. Kaliński (2008), p. 18 and 20; Warkałło (1972), pp. 112–116.

[45] Judgment of the Regional Court in Wrocław of 06 December 2018 ref. I C 1131/18, the legal nature of this relationship is controversial in the doctrine, as exemplified by the dispute in the Polish doctrine over the legal nature of a bank guarantee which is very similar in structure—cf. Dygnatowski (2015), pp. 208–214.

C. A guarantee contract involves a promise by person A to person C that B will behave in a certain way (pay the sale price, repay the loan, etc.). The guarantee contract creates a guarantee relationship between the guarantor (A) and the beneficiary (C). In contrast, the guarantee application occurs between persons B and A. The debtor (B) applies for an appropriate guarantee to the guarantor (A), who accepts it.

With regard to the above considerations concerning the insurance premium and, more broadly, the fact that the insurance guarantee is chargeable, it should be noted that the obligation to pay the premium arises from the guarantee application and not from the guarantee contract itself. Therefore, noticing that insurance guarantee is chargeable (in way of a premium or commission) is only possible by viewing it as a guarantee relationship based on tripartite relationship.

For the creditor (guarantee beneficiary), the guarantee is free of charge. The insurance guarantee contract is not regulated in European legal systems. It is an innominate contract in contrast to surety. Such a guarantee is defined as a specific, non-classified insurance transaction, shaped mainly by practice, which finds its legal basis primarily in the principle of freedom of contract. Given the lack of regulations relating to the insurance guarantee regardless of legal culture, case law plays an important role in defining this institution. The definition adopted in a decision of the Polish Supreme Court can be regarded as reflecting the legal nature of the guarantee as a tripartite relationship. It declared that „the legal meaning of an insurance guarantee is that the guarantor assumes the obligation to provide pecuniary consideration in the form of a guarantee sum in the event of a guarantee event, in particular in the event of the debtor's failure to perform its obligations under the underlying contract".[46] Any rights and obligations of the parties (i.e. the guarantor and the beneficiary) can only be based on the wording of the guarantee itself and, as a rule, cannot be defined by sources outside of it. Thus, the only source of the parties' obligations is what is included in the guarantee document (certificate). In view of this fact, it is difficult to perceive a guarantee as an act reserved for insurers only.

4 Insurance Guarantee v. Suretyship (Surety): Independence

A guarantee is one of several types of collateral. Like suretyship, it is a personal security. In both cases, a person is liable with all their assets if another person, the debtor, fails to perform a certain obligation (a secured obligation) to the creditor. Looking at its function, a guarantee is related to a suretyship. Its primary function is to secure claims for damages based on breach of contractual obligations, unilateral commitments, or promises, to secure the performance of a monetary claim arising from a legal relation.

[46] Judgement of the Supreme Court of 14 April 2016, II CSK 388/15.

A suretyship is a contract between a creditor, a principal debtor and a third party binding himself in part or in whole on behalf of the principal debtor, usually as surety and co-principal debtor. Acting on his own behalf, the surety undertakes to enter into rights and obligations of the principal debtor and pay the creditor if the principal debtor cannot. There can be no surety if there is no principal obligation. The creditor need not seek to recover the debt from the principal debtor first before enforcing the agreement against the surety. A surety is accessory in nature, which means it cannot exist without a principal obligation. In terms of civil (European continental law) law and common law, a surety is discharged if the principal obligation is extinguished, for example, due to performance by the principal debtor or to impossibility of performance or invalidity of the debt. A suretyship may also be terminated if the accessory obligation between him and the creditor is extinguished even though the principal obligation between the principal debtor and the creditor is still in force.

As a general principle guarantees create independent principal obligations while suretyships create accessory obligations. Independent guarantees developed widely in the twentieth century. At the European and international level, the terms "independent personal security"[47] or, alternatively, "independent guarantee"[48] seem to be established. The independence of this collateral is the essence of the institution. Like a suretyship, an independent guarantee is mostly based on a contractual (or another legal) relationship between a creditor and a debtor. However, in contrast to a suretyship, a guarantee is legally independent from the underlying legal relationship.

The insurance guarantee means the obligation of the guarantor (insurance company) to pay the guarantee beneficiary a specific monetary benefit in the event of a fortuitous event listed in the guarantee. In the case of an independent guarantee, the obligation of the guarantor to pay is principal in nature and exists independent of an underlying obligation or the existence of any other debt. The liability of the guarantor under a guarantee is equal to the amount, which is guaranteed (sum guaranteed). A guarantee drawing can only happen if the principal obligation or payment is completed on the part of the guarantor. A guarantee is therefore generally seen as a stronger form of security than a surety which is accessory in nature as it establishes independent liability for the principal obligation.

An insurance guarantee, in addition to a bank guarantee, is a type of independent guarantee. The only, albeit legally irrelevant, special feature of this guarantee is that the entity providing the collateral is the insurer. With a guarantee, a person (guarantor) undertakes as a self-standing principal obligation to indemnify the creditor (promisee) of another person on the happening of certain events. The guarantor's obligation is therefore independent from that of the debtor. If a creditor suffers

[47] For example, in the Principles, Definitions and Model Rules of European (DCFR), ed. von Bar et al. (2009a).

[48] For example, in the 1995 UN Convention on Independent Convention on Independent Guarantees and Stand-by Letters of Credit (in force since 1 January 2000). The Convention only applies to 'international undertakings' (Art 4) and so far it has only been ratified by eight smaller countries.

losses when it transpires that the debtor's principal contract to the creditor is invalid, the guarantor's obligation remains in force and he will have to pay those losses, (where a surety's obligation falls away and he will not have to pay anything).

The collateral value of a guarantee liability is much greater because, unlike a suretyship, the guarantor's lack of fault in failing to achieve the secured result does not release it of liability at all. The characteristic feature of a guarantee is not the takeover of the debtor's liabilities, but the assumption of the transaction risk borne by the creditor. It can therefore be concluded that the guarantor is responsible for the principal debtor, while the guarantor is responsible for achieving the guaranteed result.[49] Assumption of risk is the essence of insurance activity, which justifies the use of the insurance guarantee. A guarantee does not reinforce the underlying relationship, as does a surety, but serves to compensate the beneficiary for a loss, since the guarantor is not liable for the debtor's debt as in the case of a surety, but for obtaining a guaranteed result.[50] The contractual obligation of the debtor within guarantee liability consists of redressing of the damage by paying compensation. From the moment the guarantee contract is concluded, the creditor acquires a claim against the guarantor, which it may file against the guarantor. This claim becomes due as soon as the third party, for whose conduct the guarantee was given, fails to perform or fails to contract an obligation. This means that the effect for which the guarantee was given has not been realised.[51]

It follows from the fact that the guarantee is independent and non-accessory that the guarantor is unable to raise claims available to the debtor whose performance is covered by the guarantee against the beneficiary. In particular, it is not possible to assert statute of limitations for the principal claim (resulting from the basic legal relationship) or invoke a right of set-off against the sum covered by the guarantee. The independence of the guarantee also excludes the claim that the main contract (basic legal relationship) has not been fulfilled or has been annulled.

In the case of an environmental insurance, guarantees must be granted at the request of the waste holder when applying for a waste management permit to secure compensation claims (claims for the cost of performance related to the removal of waste from a site not intended for storage and/or the repair of environmental damage). Such performance guarantees are intended to protect the creditor (here, the environmental authority or another authority) from failure to implement an administrative decision to bear the cost of certain remedial actions.

It is worth emphasising, however, that due to the insurance guarantee contract being innominate, the above-mentioned features resulting from its independence (non-accessoriness) may be changed by the parties under the far-reaching freedom

---

[49] Spyra (2005), ABC no. 70396, Rudnicki (1999), p. 57.

[50] Resolution of the Polish Supreme Court (7 judges)—legal rule - of 16 April 1993 III CZP 16/93, judgements of the Supreme Court Sądu Najwyższego pf: 14 January 2004, I CSK 102/03, 16 April 1996, II CRN 38/96, judgement of the Court of Appeal in Katowice of 20 February 2015, V ACa 604/14, judgement of the Court of Appeal in Warsaw of 13 June 2017, I ACa 516/16.

[51] See the Resolution of 7 judges of Polish Supreme Court (legal rule) of 16 April 1993 III CZP 16/93.

of contract in this case.[52] There are no legal obstacles to the parties to a guarantee agreement to set different rules for the guarantor's liability within freedom of contract. Particularly, the guarantor's liability can be more accessory, similar to that of a guarantor. In the guarantee contract, the parties may specify circumstances excluding or limiting the liability of the insurer (guarantor). The guarantor may refuse to pay the compensation also if the guarantee beneficiary uses the security for purposes other than those stated in the guarantee (e.g. seeks to unilaterally extend the guarantee security to other underlying obligations than those provided for in the guarantee contract). The judicial decisions indicate the insurer's (guarantor) right to defend by means of a plea that the guarantee beneficiary abused the purpose of the security.[53] Hence the difficulty of distinguishing between guarantee and surety in the doctrine and combining these institutions in a single act, as it is in the common law system.

Distinguishing clearly between the concepts of non-accessoriness and abstractiveness in the context of insurance guarantees is inherently challenging, as the two notions often overlap and are used inconsistently in practice.[54] Non-accessoriness refers to the independence of the guarantor's obligation from the underlying legal relationship, whereas abstractiveness denotes a stronger form of autonomy, whereby the guarantor's obligation is performed solely on the basis of the guarantee itself. This conceptual uncertainty is generally resolved by the wording adopted in the guarantee contract. Where the contract (or the guarantee document containing the provisions of the insurance guarantee) specifies that the insurance guarantee is payable on first demand or that it is unconditional, the obligation assumes the characteristics of an abstract undertaking. In such a case, the guarantor pays the unconditional guarantee funds to the beneficiary once he submits a request for payment and fulfils the formal requirements specified in the guarantee.[55] The concepts of abstractiveness and non-accessoriness were originally developed in German law in the context of bank guarantees. Although a Versicherungsgarantie is not, and cannot be, a classical Garantie within the meaning of §§ 780–781 BGB, these theoretical categories remain useful for understanding the relationship between the two notions, particularly the nature of abstractiveness. German law offers the most precise distinction between these concepts. A classic Bürgschaft (suretyship) under §§ 765 et seq. BGB is strictly accessory, as the surety's liability depends on the existence and enforceability of the principal debtor's obligation.[561] By contrast, the Garantie constitutes an abstract promise to pay (abstraktes Schuldversprechen)

---

[52] Such possibility is indicated by the Polish Supreme Court in its judgement of 10 February 2010, V CSK 233/09.

[53] Resolution of the Polish Supreme Court of 28 April 1995 III CZP 166/94.

[54] Trzaskowski (2011), p. 210.

[55] Cf. judgement of the Polish Supreme Court of 16 December 2009, I CSK 281/09, judgement of the Court of Appeal in Łódźof 22 May 2014, I ACa 1436/13, judgement of the Regional Court in Lublinof 24 June 2015, I C 671/14).

[56] Hanns Prütting / Gerhard Wegen / Gerd Weinreich (eds), BGB Commentary (BGB Kommentar), commentary on § 765 of the Bürgerliches Gesetzbuch (German Civil Code), marginal nos. 1–5.

under §§ 780–781 BGB, the performance of which is triggered solely by the conditions set out in the guarantee itself.[57] The Bundesgerichtshof (BGH) confirmed in its landmark decision of 22 March 1984 that a "first demand guarantee" (Garantie auf erstes Anfordern) is a fully abstract obligation and that the guarantor may not refuse payment on the basis of any objections derived from the underlying relationship.[58] This jurisprudence provides a conceptual model for understanding abstractiveness: the obligation is self-standing not only in its existence, but also in its execution. While insurance guarantees do not fall within the normative scope of the BGB provisions on abstract promises and are governed instead by insurance contract law (VVG), the German distinction between accessory and abstract undertakings nevertheless sheds light on the dogmatic structure of insurance guarantees.[59]

The term "surety bond" appears to be used interchangeably with the term guarantee insurance in common law insurance legislation. Surety bond is a type of guarantee in which the surety (insurer) undertakes to cover the losses of the beneficiary (obligee) in case the principal (obligor) fails to fulfil its obligations. Usually, surety bonds are used in construction business, which also involve environmental risks. Regulators in all the major oil and gas regions of the United States, as well as Canada and other countries, have adopted some form of bond or financial security These requirements vary in stringency, with those in Texas being among the most stringent.[60] A common way to meet these requirements is to purchase an instrument called a surety bond from a private insurer at market rates. Surety bonds oblige the insurer to pay the government up to the value of the bond if the insured company goes out of business and leaves some environmental costs behind. Unlike liability insurance, if the government makes a claim on the bond, the insurer will try to recover from the oil and gas company. A surety bond therefore transfers the default risk from the insurer, who will be responsible for environmental damages that exceeds the oil and gas company's ability to pay.[61]

Palandt, Commentary on the German Civil Code (Bürgerliches Gesetzbuch – Kommentar), edited by Sprau, 83rd edition, Munich: C.H. Beck 2024, commentary on § 765 BGB, marginal nos. 2–3.

[57] Claus-Wilhelm Canaris (2023), § 28, marginal nos. 1–3.

[58] Bundesgerichtshof (Federal Court of Justice of Germany), Judgment of 22 March 1984, case no. IX ZR 66/83, published in Entscheidungen des Bundesgerichtshofs in Zivilsachen (BGHZ – Official Reports of the Decisions of the Federal Court of Justice in Civil Matters), vol. 90, p. 287.

See also Bundesgerichtshof, Judgment of 18 September 1986, case no. IX ZR 82/85, published in Neue Juristische Wochenschrift (NJW – New Legal Weekly Journal) 1987, pp. 50–51.

[59] Heiss (2017), Introduction to the Versicherungsvertragsgesetz (VVG – German Insurance Contract Act), marginal nos. 210–215 (concerning the legal nature of the Versicherungsgarantie).

[60] Dutzik Tony et al. (2013).

[61] Boomhower (2019), p. 396.

5 Insurance Guarantee vs. Insurance Contract

The term "insurance" refers to all insurance activities, i.e. both insurance contract and guarantee insurance. By contracting with a number of policyholders who want to cover similar risks, the insurer builds up a kind of pool (community) of these risks, which in turn makes it possible to use statistical methods to assess the probability of the insurer's performance of contractual obligation (understood as the payment of an indemnity or an amount of money).[62] The community of risks is fundamental to the essence of the insurance contract, as applying statistical methods and determining the probability of an insured event is the starting point for determining the premium payable to the insurer for assuming the risk, i.e. providing insurance cover. The amount of the premium is determined by assessing the likelihood of an insured event and the scale of the payout the insurer must make in case the event occurs. The possibility of using statistical and actuarial models to assess this probability presupposes, in turn, achieving an appropriate scale, which is closely linked to the concept of the community of risks. The community of risks should be perceived as the essence of insurance, as German doctrine points out in particular.[63] This is because the commonality of risks creates the possibility of determining a premium equivalent to the insurer bearing the risk, which is a necessary element of both insurance contract and guarantee insurance (treated as a legal relationship shaped by three contracts). In the absence of a community of risks that uses mathematical and statistical methods, it would be impossible to construct the premium as statistically reflecting the risk assumed by the insurer under both single insurance contract and guarantee insurance.

If we limit ourselves to the mere insurance guarantee contract concluded between the insurer and the guarantee beneficiary, we can acknowledge that such a contract differs from an insurance contract in not being reciprocal. The essence of an insurance contract is that the risk assumed by the insurer is distributed back to all insureds who participate financially by paying the premium. The premium is the equivalent of the probability of a loss occurring and, according to the leading approaches in insurance law doctrine,[64] it constitutes a counter-performance of the insured (German: Gegenleistung)[65]—corresponding to the assumption of risk by the insurance company.

However, if we look at insurance guarantee as a relationship based on three legal relationships (tripartite relationship), then this difference is no longer so clear. In particular, this applies if we refer to third party insurance or insurance taken out in

[62] Hüntemann (2008), https://d-nb.info/1008688460/34, pp. 7–9.

[63] German literature points out that mass contracting is a condition for the economic functioning of insurance—cf. Ch. Förster (2010), p. 136 and insurance literature cited. On this flavor also: A. Hüntemann—cf. A. Hüntemann (2008), p. 8.

[64] On the dispute between supporters of the monetary benefit theory and the risk theory, see more broadly Maśniak and Kamiński (2018), pp. 47–66.

[65] J. Boetius, Der Garantievertrag, …, pp. 48, 50, 52.

favor of a third party (as discussed in more detail below). As mentioned previously, such a construct corresponds to both insurance operations in question, only in the case of an insurance guarantee, the equivalence of protection is distributed between two entities: the debtor obliged to pay the premium and the beneficiary of the protection. Thus, the reference to the premium as a performance equivalent to the assumption of risk applies to both insurance contract and guarantee insurance. Even if a "commission" (not a "premium") is charged for issuing the guarantee, it is calculated taking into account the risk of the guaranteed event. Then, despite the different nomenclature, it will be close to a premium economically and conceptually.

In comparison to an insurance contract, the utmost good faith principle is modified. This principle of utmost good faith obliges both parties—the insured and the insurer—to act in good faith and give full disclosure of relevant information concerning the risk covered by the contract. Breach of this principle may result in legal consequences, including cancellation of the contract or denial of insurance claim. This rule of insurance law, according to which all material circumstances known to the insured must be disclosed, does not apply equally in the case of guarantee policies.[66] English case law has indicated that the concealment to avoid the contract of guarantee must be fraudulent, for such policies come within the law of suretyship, rather than of insurance.[67] In light of the above analyses pointing out the differences between surety and guarantee, it is difficult to agree with such a statement. A key principle of the insurance business involves the communication on risk. Such information is communicated at the contracting stage of the guarantee. The obligor is obliged to disclose all material facts that could affect the insurer's assessment of the risk (guarantor). If the obligor concealed information that could affect the risk (e.g. financial difficulties) and later defaulted on the contract, the insurer could declare the contract void for breach of the principle of utmost good faith. In this respect, it resembles the utmost good faith of the policyholder in an insurance contract. The application of this principle to the insurer involves the obligation to provide clear and transparent terms and conditions, act in accordance with the best interests of the customer, and the ban of misselling, which is explicitly referred to in the EU IDD directive (Art. 17).[68] Although the directive does not refer to an insurance guarantee, there are pre-contractual obligations related to insurance products (as an insurance guarantee should be considered an insurance product, just like with an insurance contract) introduced by the directive: the analysis of requirements and needs as well as the delivery of a standardised document providing information on the insurance product. This is evidenced by the implementation of these provisions into national legal orders, where, for example, the obligation to analyse the requirements and needs of the customer should precede the conclusion of insurance or insurance guarantee contract (see Art. 8 of the Polish Insurance Distribution Act). Particularly,

66 N. British Insurance v. Lloyd, Io Ex. 523, 24 L. J. Ex. 14. Seaton v. Burnand (1900), App. Cas. 135.

67 Ravenscroft v. Provident Clerks', &c., 5 Times L. R. 3. Liverpool Starr Bowkett, &c. v. Travellers' Accident, 9 Times L. R. 221.

68 Bagińska (2019), pp. 15–17; Malinowska (2008), pp. 159–185.

this applies to the insurance guarantee contract concluded between the insurer (as guarantor) and the guarantee beneficiary. However, one should consider applying these requirements to the relationship between the guarantor (as insurer) and the debtor (obligor/prinicipal).

The difference with respect to the bilateral relationship arising from an insurance contract is the absence or very limited application of the principle of utmost good faith in the guarantee beneficiary. A further question also arises as to whether, in the context of a waste guarantee, the principle of utmost good faith might manifest itself in the relationship between the guarantor (insurer) and the public authority whose body issues the environmental decision. The issuance of such a decision constitutes an event listed in the guarantee, and the guarantor's actual and legal obligation depends on the legality of that administrative act. This raises the issue of whether the guarantor thereby acquires a legal interest to challenge the act and whether all remedies available to the party to whom the decision is addressed (the waste holder) should likewise be accessible to the guarantor.

In common law doctrine, the insurance contract is identified as the most common case of indemnity.[69] The similarity is that the insurer—just as the indemnity debtor—undertakes to pay in case a specified event occurs. There is a noticeable difference between indemnity and guarantee in terms of the ultimate allocation of the economic burden of the obligation. As the guarantee is intended to secure performance by the principal debtor, the guarantor who has satisfied the creditor may have a recourse or subrogation claim against the principal debtor. The entitlement to such a claim does not apply to indemnification, since in this case the debtor definitively assumes the risk of performance due to the materialisation of a specific risk.[70] The insurer's recourse claim against the debtor (obligor) is the most important difference between an insurance contract and an insurance guarantee, affecting the level of the insurance risk assumed by the insurer, which translates into the insurance premium. The possibility to assert a recourse claim against the obligor allows the guarantee commission/premium to be shaped at a lower level than the premium in the insurance contract.

From the point of view of the use of insurance for waste management, personal insurances or fixed sum insurances[71] (according to the classification adopted in PEICL) are outside the scope of interest. The comparison of the insurance guarantee refers to a comparison with property insurance contracts and, according to the classification adopted in PEICL—indemnity insurance (Articles 8:101 -12:102 of PEICL).

The term "indemnity insurance" is used to describe insurance contracts provided by insurers to cover the risk of policyholders suffering damage. Upon the occurrence of an insured event, the insurer is responsible for settling the claim for

[69] Courtney (2014), p. 4.

[70] Cf. Judgement of the English High Court, Queen's Bench Division vs. *Dane v. Mortgage Insurance Ltd* [1894], 1 QB, s. 54 et seq., cit. per P.J. Booth, Booth (2015), p. 9.

[71] Only personal insurance (life, health, accident and similar insurance) may be taken out as insurances of fixed sums (Article 13:101 PEICL).

damages actually suffered by the policyholder. Indemnity insurance policies are therefore designed to compensate the policyholder for actually incurred damages. This compensatory function differentiates indemnity insurance policies from fixed-sum insurance policies. The latter type of insurance stipulates that the policyholder, in the event of a claim, receives the insurance sum that has been contractually agreed upon in advance. The question of whether damage has been sustained is irrelevant for the payment of the sum insured. This distinction regarding indemnity and fixed sum insurance is worth considering when comparing insurance contract and guarantee insurance. The guarantor's liability is not compensatory in nature, as its purpose is to achieve a given result and not to redress a damage. This liability arises regardless of, or in spite of the damage. The beneficiary does not have to prove damage while exercising a claim under the guarantee.[72] This means that the insurer's liability is not regarded as a liability for damages with all the consequences following. The compensatory nature of indemnity insurance contract results in the lack of possibility to cover risks whose materialisation do not result in a damage. An example of such a risk is the closure of a landfill site and/or relocation to another site, treated as a risk. For such case, the Landfil directive requires financial security (Article 8(a)(iv)). The indicated difference between the two insurance instruments shows the advantage of an insurance guarantee as a possible financial security in such a case. It should be noted, that the failure to achieve the expected result secured by the guarantee contract constitutes a loss for the beneficiary, compensated by the payment of the guarantee sum. Although its payment does not constitute a typical compensation, it fulfils an compensatory function.[73]

Practice and legislation seem to vary considerably from country to country, and this is reflected in differing doctrinal qualifications.[74] It is sometimes difficult to distinguish between insurance contract and guarantee insurance, particularly where insurance contract is not specifically regulated (see England). There is no doubt that the same risks can be hedged by both institutions, which is the key consideration of this study—utilising them in waste management. A guarantee provides security in the event of liquidity loss/insolvency of the debtor. A financial insurance contract, in which the insurer undertakes to cover costs caused by the liquidity loss/insolvency of the insuring debtor, can play the same role. Within the area of interest, precisely these two insurance instruments take on particular significance as means of financial security of claims to cover damages related to the environmental consequences of waste management. The key difference between the two comes down to the bilateral or tripartite nature of the established relationships. In the case of an insurance contract, the relationship involves only the insured debtor and the insurer. By contrast, in the case of a guarantee, the protection beneficiary (the creditor) becomes a party to the guarantee contract. This affects the legal nature of the relationship, directly involving a third party. In the case of insuring the costs imposed

[72] Jakubecki et al. (2000), p. 75.

[73] Koch (2011), p. 653.

[74] von Bar et al. (2009b), p. 1133.

by environmental authorities in case of damage caused by waste holders, the problem is the inability of the environmental authority, which is outside the insurance legal relationship, to influence the content of the insurance conditions shaping the scope of coverage.

Introducing a third party into the insurance relationship established by an insurance contract is possible by means of an Insurance in favor of a third party. An insurance relationship in which the policyholder and the insured are two different entities is regulated in the PEICL. According to Article 11:101, "Entitlement of the Insured (1) In the case of an insurance taken out for a person other than the policyholder, if the insured event occurs, that person shall be entitled to the insurance money". An insurance in favor of a third party is sometimes confused with an insurance guarantee. It is evidenced by case law, indicating that in business transactions it is sometimes not easy to determine the legal nature of the legal relationship established with the insurer.[75] Both solutions are characterised by the establishment of a relationship involving three parties. Therefore, they may in practice constitute alternative solutions in situations involving several cooperating entities, as is the case with waste management. The same objective may be achieved by means of an insurance guarantee and an insurance in favor of a third party—in the case of the discussed relationship between the waste holder and the administrative authority issuing the waste management permit, while at the same time requiring adequate financial security, In the insurance in favor of a third party, this objective is achieved by means of a single contract in which the policyholder and the insured are two different entities. As the policyholder is obliged to pay the premium, it would be the waste holder. In such a contract, the insured would be the administrative authority (environmental authority). An insurance in favor of a third party consists in the insurance of someone else's property interest (in the subject case, the interest of the administrative authority) by the waste holder insurer acting on its own behalf. The insurer, by paying compensation to the administrative authority, fulfils its obligation. However, the obligation results in the waste holder's liability for the waste holder's debt towards the administrative authority—i.e. for someone else's debt. In contrast, in the case of a guarantee, the obliged insurer, as guarantor, pays its own debt if certain circumstances arise (for example, a decision to use the security funds for land reclamation is issued). Applying an insurance guarantee in the subject cases would lead to a similar effect as insurance in favor of a third party. There would, however, be differences arising from the treatment of the debtor (here the waste holder), who is bound to the guarantor (insurer) by a legal relationship arising from the guarantee application.

In the case of a guarantee used as a financial security instrument for the beneficiary, its attractiveness lies in the fact that any improper performance of the contractual relationship between the principal debtor and the guarantor does not affect the scope of the guarantor's liability towards the beneficiary. This stands in contrast to

[75] Cf. Judgement of the Polish Supreme Court of 16 December 2003 SN II CK 330/02; not published.

liability insurance, where—for example—non-payment of the premium, termination of the insurance contract, withdrawal from it, or, in an extreme scenario, the invalidity of the contract results in the potential injured party having no claim against the insurer. This is because such a claim is derived solely from the insurance contract and does not arise from an autonomous right held by the injured party vis-à-vis the insurer (i.e., the guarantor-insurer). In other words, what is crucial is not simply that the legal structure is tripartite per se, but whether the beneficiary derives its entitlement to claim against the guarantor/insurer from its own substantive right, or only as a derivative of the principal debtor's right (e.g., the waste holder). For this reason, although the same economic objective may indeed be achieved through insurance taken out for the benefit of a third party, from the perspective of the beneficiary this construction entails greater legal risk than a guarantee. If such insurance were to satisfy the beneficiary's legal and economic interest, then the beneficiary—this time as the "insured" under an insurance in favor of a third party—would need to be granted access to information enabling continuous monitoring of the validity and effectiveness of the security. This would include, inter alia, information on premium payments, continuity of coverage, and any contractual mechanisms allowing the insurer or the policyholder to terminate or withdraw from the contract.

6 Insurance Guarantee vs. Bank Guarantee

The construct of an insurance guarantee largely resembles that of a bank guarantee.[76] Hence, the legislation treats both guarantees as equivalent means of securing receivables, as exemplified by the waste management regulations. The bank guarantee is regulated more often, an example of which are the regulations included in the Polish Banking Law Act.[77] Some judicial decisions include statements that due to the lack of a separate statutory regulation concerning an insurance guarantee, the rules concerning a statutorily regulated bank guarantee are relevant.[78]

In many cases, the waste holder, as an entrepreneur with established banking relationships, may be able to obtain a credit limit from banks. However, a key practical issue is that banks typically treat the potential liability arising from a bank

[76] Koch (2011), p. 611.

[77] Article 81 of the Banking Law Act of29 August 1997, Polish Journal of Laws of 2024, item 1646, 1685, 1863, and of 2025 item 146.- "the bank guarantee is a unilateral obligation of the bank-guarantor that once the entity has fulfilled the entitled (guarantee beneficiary) specified conditions of payment, which may be identified as specified in this provision of documents, which the beneficiary annexes to the payment claim drawn up in the form indicated, the bank will carry out a cash benefit to the beneficiary of the guarantee either directly or indirectly through another bank".

[78] Judgement of the Polish Supreme Court of 15 February 2018, IV CSK 86/17, Legalis, and the judgement of the Polish Supreme Court of 10 February 2010, V CSK 233/09, OSNC 2010, No. 11, item 146, explicitly stated that "the features of an insurance guarantee are similar to a bank guarantee".

guarantee as equivalent to a credit exposure. As a result, a bank guarantee becomes an economically burdensome instrument for entrepreneurs, as it effectively reduces their credit capacity in the same way as a loan. By contrast, the significant advantage of an insurance guarantee is that it does not place a burden on the entrepreneurs' bank credit lines. The insurance guarantee facility leaves their bank credit lines available for working capital and other funding needs, allowing for a more cost-efficient management of their corporate debt. It constitutes an additional source of finance, complementary to bank financing. For entrepreneurs, diversifying financial instruments is essential in order to avoid the operational risk associated with dependence on a single financial institution. This aspect becomes particularly important in the situation of a waste holder's need to obtain compulsory financial security. In case the waste holder is heavily indebted, it may not be possible to obtain a bank guarantee, or it may involve a high cost for the waste holder's entrepreneur ordering the guarantee.

7 Insurance Guarantee v. Security Deposit: Function

The primary function of an insurance guarantee (as with other types of guarantees) is to secure a claim. In this sense, it is, in a way, a substitute for a security deposit and hence should be equally effective. The payment of a security deposit gives the creditor the possibility to satisfy his claims easily and quickly, but does not determine if use of the security deposit is legitimate in each case and the claims actually exist. In the economic sense, a guarantee is intended to serve a similar function to that of a security deposit. A creditor who received a security deposit can simply keep it if he argues to have a claim against the debtor, but this fact does not determine if he actually has such a claim. Consequently, the debtor can then claim the return of the security deposit if it was wrongfully retained. Similarly, the "drawing on the guarantee" by the beneficiary and receiving the payment from the guarantor does not at all determine the fact that the transfer of assets was legitimate and, in particular, that the creditor had a claim which was secured by the guarantee. Unlike a security deposit, it does not require the debtor to freeze the money, while at the same time it is intended to provide the creditor with protection comparable to that which it would have enjoyed had the money been deposited by the debtor.

It was stated in the case law that the primary function of a guarantee is to replace a security deposit.[79] The purpose of a guarantee contract is to provide the beneficiary with a secure and easily realisable guarantee of performance by the specified debtor. From this point of view, the significance of the guarantee lies not only in protecting the beneficiary against the risk of insolvency of his counterparty, but also against the risk of long and difficult pursuing of claims.[80] The legal literature also

[79] Judgement of the Court of Appeal in Katowice of 11 March 2014, V ACa 781/13, Legalis.

[80] Judgement of the Court of Appeal in Warsaw of 9.7.2013, I ACa 48/13, Legalis.

compares an insurance (or bank) guarantee to a security deposit, arguing that the guarantee has evolved precisely to replace the security deposit, which has the obvious inconvenience of freezing capital.[81] It is noted that the international success of this type of security is due to the fact that the beneficiary can have a certainty.[82]

The characteristics of the guarantor–insurer, together with the legally safeguarded solvency requirements imposed by the Solvency II Directive, indicate that an insurance guarantee may be regarded as a substitute for a cash deposit. The risk margin associated with the potential insolvency of the insurer should not alter this assessment, as this form of financial security does not immobilise funds that could otherwise be used for investment purposes. From a macroeconomic perspective, the public interest therefore clearly favours the choice of an insurance guarantee over a cash deposit, even when taking into account the hypothetical risk of insurer insolvency. It should also be noted that a cash deposit is paid into a bank account, making the beneficiary merely a creditor entitled to the payment of funds held in that account; the funds are not physically stored in a vault in the form of traditional cash. In practice, this means that a cash deposit likewise carries the risk of bank insolvency and uncertainty as to the scope of protection afforded to bank deposits.

References

Bagińska E (2019) Wpływ klauzul generalnych na proces zawierania umowy ubezpieczenia w świetle ustawy o dystrybucji ubezpieczeń. Wiadomości Ubezpieczeniowe (Insurance Review), No 3/2019

Boetius J (1966) Der Garantievertrag. Inaugural-Dissertation zur Erlangung der Doktorwürde einer Hohen Juristischen Fakultät der Ludwig-Maximilians-Universität zu München, München, p 15

Boomhower J (2019) Drilling like there's no tomorrow. Am Econ Rev 109(2):396

Booth PJ (2015) Problems with contractual indemnities (and how to avoid them). Victorian Bar. March

Canaris C-W (2023) Bank contract law (Bankvertragsrecht), 4th edn. C.H. Beck, Munich

Courtney W (2014), Contractual indemnities. Hart, Oxford

Dygnatowski W (2015) Wybrane zagadnienia dotyczące charakteru prawnego gwarancji bankowej na tle doktryny i nauki prawa. Roczniki Administracji i Prawa nr XV(1)

Förster C (2010) Die Fusion von Bürgschaft und Garantie: Eine Neusystematisierung aus rechtsvergleichender Perspektive. Tübingen

Garner BA (2019) Black's law dictionary, 11th edn. Claitor's Pub Division

Grossman SJ (1981) The informational role of warranties. J Law Econ 24(3). Consumer Protection Regulation: A Conference Sponsored by the Center for the Study of the Economy and the State, The University of Chicago Press

Heiss H (2017) Munich commentary on the insurance contract act (Münchener Kommentar zum Versicherungsvertragsgesetz), 2nd edn. C.H. Beck, Munich

Hüntemann A (2008) Der Abschluss von Versicherungsverträgen und die vorvertraglichen Pflichten des Versicherers gemäß §§ 6 und 7 VVG. Inaugural-Dissertation zur Erlangung des

[81] Cf. Pokrzywniak (2020) Legalis, Tracz (1998), p. 103; Koch (2011), p. 623.

[82] Pyziak-Szafnicka (1994), p. 17.

akademischen Grades eines Doktors der Rechte durch die Rechtswissenschaftliche Fakultät der Westfälischen Wilhelms-Universität zu Münster. https://d-nb.info/1008688460/34
Jakubecki A, Mojak J, Niezbecka E (2000) Prawne zabezpieczenie wierzytelności bankowych. Wolters Kluwer
Jastrzębski J (2018) Nieubezpieczeniowe umowy gwarancyjne. PPH 7:4–15
Jastrzębski J (2021) Umowa gwarancyjna. Warszawa
Kaliński M (2008) Szkoda na mieniu i jej naprawienie. C.H. Beck
Kleiner B (1979) Bankgarantie. Die Garantie unter besonderer Berücksichtigung des Bankgarantiegeschäftes. Zürich
Koch A (2011) System Prawa Prywatnego, Prawo zobowiązań – część szczegółowa, tom 8, Wolters Kluwer
Łętowska E (1970) Umowa o świadczenie przez osobę trzecią. Warszawa
Malinowska K (2008) Umowa ubezpieczenia w Europie bez granic. Oficyna Wydawnicza Branta, Bydgoszcz-Poznań
Maśniak D, Kamiński Ł (2018) Spór o ryzyko w naukach prawnych i jego skutki prawne. In: Zalewski W (ed) Pojęcie ryzyka a przestępczość ubezpieczeniowa. Wydawnictwo Arche, Sopot
Netter E (2010) Les garanties indemnitaires. Droit. Université de Strasbourg
Pokrzywniak J (2020) Umowa gwarancji ubezpieczeniowej. In: M. Stec (ed) Prawo umów handlowych. System Prawa Prywatnego. Tom 5b, Warszawa
Pyziak-Szafnicka M (1994) Gwarancja autonomiczna. Przegląd Prawa Handlowego 2
Rabel E (1950) The nature of warranty of quality. Tul Law Rev 24:277
Radin M (1929) Guaranty and Suretyship. Calif Law Rev 17(6):605
Rudnicki S (1999) Zabezpieczenia majątkowe wierzytelności pieniężnych. Zielona Góra
Spyra T (2005) Charakter prawny gwarancji bankowej. ABC no. 70396
Tony D, Davis B, Heeke TY (2013) Who pays the cost of fracking? Weak bonding rules for oil and gas drilling leave the public at risk. John Rumpler Environment America Research & Policy Center, Denver
Tracz G (1998) Umowa gwarancji ze szczególnym uwzględnieniem gwarancji bankowej. Wolters Kluwer, Kraków
Trzaskowski R (2011) Poręczenie i gwarancja bankowa. Warszawa
von Bar C, Clive E, Schulte-Nölke H, Beale H, Herre J, Huet J, Storme M, Swann S, Varul P, Veneziano A, Zoll F (2009a) Principles, Definitions and Model Rules of European (DCFR)
von Bar C, Clive E, Schulte-Nölke H, Beale H, Herre J, Huet J, Storme M, Swann S, Varul P, Veneziano A, Zol F (2009b) Principles, definitions and model rules of european private law draft common frame of reference (DCFR). European Law Publishers
Warkałło W (1972) *Odpowiedzialność* odszkodowawcza. Funkcje, rodzaje, granice. Warszawa

Subject, Coverage and Distribution of Waste Insurance

1 Introduction

This chapter is devoted to an analysis of the subject matter, scope of cover and distribution of insurance relating to waste management. The chapter aims to systematise and assess the insurance instruments currently operating on the insurance market insofar as they are used to address risks arising from waste-related activities, taking into account both their legal construction and the regulatory environment in which they function.

The chapter opens with an examination of the insurability of waste-related risks, considered in light of the classical criteria developed in insurance law and insurance economics. This is followed by an analysis of insurable interest in waste insurance, with particular attention paid to the specific characteristics of waste management activities and to the coexistence of multiple insurance interests that may arise in this context, including those of waste holders, private parties affected by environmental damage, and public entities responsible for environmental protection.

Subsequently, the chapter addresses liability insurance as the traditional legal mechanism for providing insurance protection against environmental damage connected with waste management. The analysis encompasses both general civil liability insurance and specialised forms of environmental liability insurance, with particular emphasis on the role of pollution exclusion clauses and their interpretation in case law. This part of the chapter highlights the structural limits of liability-based insurance protection when applied to waste-related environmental risks.

Against this background, the chapter proceeds to examine first-party insurance solutions, including environmental cost insurance, as instruments that may complement or, in certain respects, substitute liability insurance. The discussion focuses on the function of these insurance products, their scope of coverage and their relevance for financing preventive and remedial measures in the field of waste management.

D. Maśniak, *The Legal Framework for the Use of Insurance in Ecological Waste Management*, AIDA Europe Research Series on Insurance Law and Regulation 17, https://doi.org/10.1007/978-3-032-26550-0_6

The chapter also addresses issues related to the distribution of waste insurance, taking into account the regulatory framework governing insurance distribution and the specific position of waste insurance within that framework. Particular attention is paid to the role of insurance distributors in identifying and responding to the demands and needs of waste holders, which are often shaped by binding legal and administrative requirements rather than solely by economic considerations.

Finally, the chapter examines the position of the environmental authority, which, although remaining formally outside the insurance relationship, plays a significant role in its formation, supervision and practical operation. This analysis illustrates the interaction between private-law insurance arrangements and public-law regulatory mechanisms that characterise insurance solutions applied in the area of waste management.

2 Insurability of Waste Risk

Insurability is a term of art in insurance economics and insurance practice. Its purpose is to denote the minimum requirements a certain category of risk must satisfy in order to be eligible for coverage. The requirements of insurability are expressed differently in several treatises on insurance economics.[1] Most of the differences are of terminological nature alone, as there is a common core of requirements. In order to be insurable, a particular risk must be: (a) accidental (b) determinable and measurable (c) independent (d) non-catastrophic.[2] However, it is emphasised in the doctrine that the requirements are met to their fullest extent in hardly any kind of insurance. Hence insurability is decidedly a soft concept which lends itself to an assessment in terms of more-or-less instead of either/or decisions.[3]

The requirement that the risk be accidental responds to the contingency that losses may be caused by the insured himself. To the extent this is the case, the insured has the power to release the insurer from the obligation at his will. This is the reason why the insurance law excludes intentional torts from the scope of coverage of third party insurance.[4] Since insureds normally retain at least some influence on the probability and severity of loss, the element of accidentalness is never satisfied in full. Although intentional torts are routinely excluded from insurance cover, loss caused by negligence is not. Negligence involves conscious behaviour, and the frequency and severity of loss is not entirely independent of the conscious decisions of the insured. Therefore, most risks covered by liability insurance are not accidental to their full extent. Experience shows that it is even possible to insure "risks" that

[1] Rejda (2017), p. 21.
[2] Wagner (2007), p. 89.
[3] Wagner (2007), p. 91.
[4] Cf., e.g. § 152 of the German Contract of Insurance Act (Versicherungsvertragsgesetz).

are not at all accidental, as in the case of insuring a hotel after it has burned down.[5] This example allows to consider insurability the risk of landfill or waste facility closure before the planned date for doing so. However, even not so rigorous interpretation of the *accidental* requirement raises serious difficulties when using an insurance contract as a requirement for the operator "to ensure that all the obligations flowing from the permit are fulfilled, including those relating to the closure procedure and after-care of the site" (motive 28 Landfill Directive). This requirement also prevents graduał pollution caused by environmentally harmful waste management from being treated as an insured accident covered by insurance.[6]

In order to create a profitable venture by concluding an insurance contract, the insurer must first be able to calculate the premium to be paid by the insuring party. This in turn requires the actuarial value of the risk in question to be known. The insurer must have information concerning both the frequency and the severity of losses. Collecting such data is only possible if the insured event is well-defined and may be determined with reasonable certainty in the case it materialises. Unlike the so-called traditional types of insurance, little information has been collected on the frequency and severity of losses in the case of waste risks insurance coverage. There are also no reliable statistics available. The effects of pollution are often immeasurable and irreversible. The development of high-speed technology brings new sectors with waste risks every day, also adding to the difficulties in measuring the risks.[7] Claims that risks must be identifiable and measurable to be insurable, however, are rare in insurance practice. Although not well defined, waste risks are not impossible to define. Even where an insurable event is identifiable with reasonable certainty, the problem of calculation remains. The idea of really 'calculating' a premium with a reasonable degree of precision seems very difficult to realize.

In order to be insurable, risks must be independent rather than cumulative. The requirement of independence follows from the feature of insurance as a mechanism of pooling similar risks. If an insurer pools together waste risks of 10,000 waste holders, the uncertainty about the number and severity of accidents disappears. Let's suppose that the statistics reveal that 10,000 waste holders are expected to cause losses amounting to X euros per year. A contrasting situation would be one in which there is protection of property interests from risks which, if materialised, would affect them all. The doctrine indicates flood threatening entrepreneurs operating along the banks of a major river as an example of such a situation. An insurer who has covered coastal owners remains unscathed in years without flooding. However, when such an event occurs, all insured will be affected at the same time. The insurer's contractual obligation will be close to the two extremes, i.e. either zero or the maximum. Pollution caused by waste management can hardly be compared to such a situation. However, it is possible to imagine a cumulative risk due to

---

[5] Smith and Witt (1985), p. 379.

[6] Examples of extensive gradual pollution causing a sequence of environmental damage cf. Wettersteinn (1997), pp. 29–30.

[7] Faure and Liu (2018), p. 259.

the use of a specific material by multiple producers, the environmental impact of which is unknown at the time the insurance cover is provided. An insurer that would assume the risk of having such a waste, in effect takes a bet on the safety of that type of product. If the waste turned out to be harmless, the insurance cover would be unnecessary. However, if it turned out to be harmful (e.g., like asbestos) the insurer's liability would increase from zero to a maximum. Cumulative risk affects whole series of products.

Environmental damage caused by waste risks can be described as catastrophic in the sense that coverage of the losses can exhaust insurers' financial resources. Losses that are manageable on a case-by-case basis accumulate to unmanageable losses because many people are negatively affected at the same time by the same damaging event. Environmental damage affecting elements of the environment: rivers, soil, animal life and human health caused by low-level management of hazardous waste can lead to disaster, especially in the case of waste with particularly harmful properties. Even very large risks which are often the result of an accumulation of individual ones may be easily insured, albeit partially. In the real world, hardly any insurance product is offered without any limit.

Taken together, the foregoing analysis demonstrates that waste-related risks only partially satisfy the classical requirements of insurability and do so in a markedly imperfect manner. Accidentalness, measurability, independence and non-catastrophic character are present only to a limited extent and often remain subject to significant uncertainty. This confirms that insurability in the context of waste risks must be understood as a flexible and relative concept rather than as a strict threshold condition. These structural limitations do not, however, preclude the use of insurance as a risk management tool; instead, they shape the scope, structure and distribution of waste insurance products. Consequently, the imperfect insurability of waste risks has direct implications for the definition of insurable interest, the design of liability and first-party insurance coverage, the role of exclusions and limitations, and the mechanisms of insurance distribution.

3 Insurable Interest in Waste Insurance

According to the theory of insurable interest[8] the subject of insurance is the interest that a certain person has in a certain thing not being destroyed or damaged. Generally, insurable interest is understood as a special type of legal interest.[9] The object of insurance is not the thing itself, but the right held over it, i.e. the interest held in its preservation in good condition and adequate value. From the point of view of the

[8] More broadly on the theory of insurance interest see Byczko (2013), pp. 71–75.

[9] According to the generally accepted definition by V. Ehrenberg (the creator of the classical form of this concept)—insurance interest means "the relationship of a person to an object that may cause a pecuniary loss to that person as a result of an event that may occur with the object in question".—V. Ehreneberg, Versicherungsrecht, Lepipzig 1893, p. 286 cit. per Kowalewski (1997), p. 77.

legal nature of the insurance contract, the concept of insurable interest is most often considered in terms of the object of insurance, treated as an equivalent of risk. The two concepts (risk and interest) are functionally linked and constitute the essence of insurance treated as an instrument of protection.[10] The concept of insurable interest can be defined in four ways: (1) as a property that the insured loses in the event of an accident, (2) as the monetary value of such property, (3) as the benefit that the insured gets if the contractually stipulated accident does not occur, and (4) as the need to protect against a certain risk.[11]

The importance of the insurable interest becomes clear in terms of the legal variants of the insurance contract. Protection can be offered for a specific type of interest: owner, holder, creditor. Different persons may have interests concerning the same asset. The permissibility for a person to insure not only their own interest but also the interest of another person on the basis of insurance for a third party's benefit is also not questioned. Such insurance is commonly referred to as a contract in favour or on account of a third party.[12] In property insurance, the injured party is the person who suffers damage as a result of the accident and for whom the damage means an infringement of his/her insurance interest. In the case of insuring the costs of substitutive performance of preventive and remedial measures resulting from a decision of an authority (administrative body), it can be assumed that the injured insured person is the waste holder because the substitutive performance occurred as a result of his failure to take the required measures as a potential polluter. It also reasonable to consider the existence of an insurable interest on the part of the public entity represented by the environmental authority issuing the administrative decision and ordering the implementation of preventive and remedial measures. It would then be possible to consider the conclusion of an insurance contract by a waste holder (e.g. a landfill manager) in favour of a public entity (e.g. the State Treasury or a local authority). The choice of the type of insurance contract is important insofar as compensation constituting a way of redressing the damage should be paid to the injured party. The entity that incurred or is obliged to incur the costs of prevention and/or removal of pollution and restoration of the environment is the injured party.[13]

Insurance for a third party's benefit can respond to objections to the concept of environmental first party insurance, in which the injured party is both the insured and the policyholder obliged to pay the premium. Paying the costs of such insurance cover is seen as contradicting the polluter-pays principle (discussed more broadly in the second chapter). The insurance for a third party's benefit allows the potentially polluting waste holder to be charged for the insurance premium while naming the

[10] Kowalewski (1997), p. 73.

[11] Kisch (1933).

[12] See Chapter 11 of PEICL: Insured Persons other than the Policyholder-Principles of European Insurance Contract Law (PICL), ed. Basedow et al. (2016), p. 267 et seq.

[13] Cf. Żebrowska (1997), p. 3.

injured party (e.g. the public entity ordering the prevention and remediation measures) as the insured.

It should be emphasised that the same factual sphere may simultaneously give rise to several distinct insurable interests, which in turn may be protected by different insurance contracts, without any contradiction between them. In particular, the existence of a liability insurance covering damage caused to third parties does not exclude the possibility of concluding a property insurance contract protecting the injured party's own interest. Likewise, where insurance is taken out for the benefit of a third party, this does not preclude the policyholder from insuring its own losses or costs under a separate contract concluded for its own account. This multiplicity of insurable interests and contractual constructions is of particular importance in the context of waste-related risks, where environmental damage, regulatory obligations and economic losses may overlap but do not necessarily coincide in legal terms. The essence of insurance lies precisely in the fact that the scope of the insurer's obligation is determined by the insured interest and the contractual allocation of risk, rather than by the concept of damage alone. Consequently, the existence of parallel insurance arrangements protecting different interests—whether of the waste holder, the injured public authority, or other affected entities—should be regarded as a functional feature of insurance law. Recognising this specificity is indispensable for a proper understanding of waste insurance structures, particularly where insurance mechanisms are expected to complement public-law environmental liability regimes.

4 Liability Insurance for Waste

4.1 Waste Risk as the Content of a Pollution Exclusion in the Business-Related Liability Insurance in the Light of US Case Law

An analysis of US case law indicates that attempts are being made to pursue claims for waste management damages under Commercial General Liability Insurance (CGL) within general liability insurance. Commercial General Liability (CGL[14]) insurance in the US covers two main areas of liability: premises liability (liability for damage to persons and property) and product liability.[15]

[14] CGL policies were designed by the Insurance Services Office (ISO), standardised in the 1940s and amended many times since then. CGL policies, as general liability policies, indemnify the insured for legal liabilities incurred by the insured for third-party claims for bodily injury and property damage and other harms such as personal and advertising injury caused by acts or omissions of the insured.

[15] See Bailey Kathy and Gulledge (1997), pp. 26–30.

Most CGL (Commercial General Liability Insurance) policies available in the US insurance market adopt pollution exclusion language in their policies that is similar to the language used in the standard Insurance Services Office form,[16] as evidenced by definitions adopted by insurers involved in litigation. "Pollutants" are defined in the policy as "any solid, liquid, gaseous or thermal irritant or contaminant, including smoke, vapor, soot, fumes, acids, alkalis, chemicals and waste"[17]; Waste includes material to be recycled, reconditioned or reclaimed."[18];. As can be seen, in all conditions "waste" is treated as a "pollutant" excluded from the scope of protection.[19]

The highest courts in California, Illinois, and Louisiana all determined that the pollution exclusion was ambiguous. These courts developed three separate interpretations of pollution under the absolute pollution exclusion. Although the California Supreme Court attempted to provide a uniform interpretation of the absolute pollution exclusion, lower courts in California have not always utilized this interpretation. One of the lower California courts circumvented the supreme court's interpretation by finding the pollution exclusion clause unambiguous, which required a very different analysis from that used by the Supreme Court.[20]

The importance of the problem identified is highlighted by an analysis of the case Ortega Rock Quarry v. Golden Eagle Insurance Corp., where a California appeals court interpreted an absolute pollution exclusion clause. Ortega Rock Quarry requested indemnification and defense from its insurance provider for claims arising out of an Environmental Protection Agency ("EPA") order and lawsuit that arose from the fact that Ortega placed fill dirt and rocks along an access road that later discharged into a creek. The insurance company denied coverage for the action under the absolute pollution exclusion because, it argued, dirt and rocks were pollutants. The court determined that the pollution exclusion was not ambiguous and denied coverage for the claim. In reaching this conclusion, however, the court never explicitly explained why dirt and rocks could be commonly thought of as pollution. The lower court's decision in Ortega Rock Quarry case also reveals the problem that can arise when lower courts do not apply the interpretation suggested by the state supreme court. When the lower court failed to apply the supreme court's interpretation of pollution, the expectation gap increased because both insureds and insurance providers became uncertain about whether the supreme court's test would be used by lower courts in the future. After finding that the pollution exclusion is ambiguous, courts should apply a three-factor analysis to determine if an alleged pollutant is, in fact, pollution, which would then trigger the application of the CGL's

---

[16] Meeks (2009), p. 828.

[17] See, Bituminous Cas. Corp. v. Sand Livestock Sys., Inc., 728 N.W.2d 216 219 (Iowa 2007); Nav-Its, Inc. v. Selective Ins. Co., 869 A.2d 929, 932 (N.J. 2005).

[18] Clendenin Bros. v. United States Fire Insurance, 889 A.2d.

[19] Cf. insurance terms and conditions referred to in the case MacKinnon v. Truck Ins. Exch., 31 Cal. 4th 635, 644 (2003).

[20] See Ortega Rock Quarry v. Golden Eagle Ins. Corp., 46 Cal. Rptr. 3d 517, 527-32 (Cal. Ct. App. 2006). But see Garamendi v. Golden Eagle Ins. Co., 25 Cal. Rptr. 3d 642, 646 (Cal. Ct. App. 2005).

pollution exclusion. The three factors are (1) whether the alleged pollutant is mainly natural or chemical in origin, (2) whether the alleged pollutant is typically hazardous in the way it caused the harm, and (3) whether the insured is typically a polluter.

In Ortega Rock Quarry case, the alleged pollution occurred when a rock quarry released rocks and dirt into a creek to maintain an access road that was washed out when the creek flooded. As a preliminary matter, the court first found that the pollution exclusion is ambiguous so that the court applied the proposed three-factor analysis of pollution. First, the court would consider the composition of the alleged pollution to determine whether it was natural or chemical in origin. In this case, the first factor is easily determined because rocks and dirt are natural materials. In fact, this is an abnormally clear case because the rocks and dirt at issue did not contain any potential chemical material. Because the alleged pollutant consists of natural materials, this factor suggests that the alleged pollutant falls outside the pollution exclusion's definition of pollution. Next, the court would apply the second factor of the test: whether the alleged pollutant is typically hazardous in the way it caused the harm. In this case, the rocks and dirt were hazardous in the way they caused the harm. Here, the fact that rocks filled the creek is the harm, and this is the exact harm that insureds and insurers would have contemplated when deciding whether rocks could be hazardous pollution. This is thus unlike a case where a toxic chemical was hazardous because of the harm it could cause if ingested, but instead caused harm because it was wet and someone slipped on it. In this case, the parties likely understood that the reason that rocks can pollute is because the rocks could interfere with a waterway, and the rocks were thus actually hazardous in this case for that reason-because they filled the creek. This factor, therefore, would suggest finding of pollution under the pollution exclusion.

Finally, in Ortega Rock Quarry Case, the court would apply the third factor: whether the insured was a polluter. In this case, the insured operated a rock quarry. A rock quarry is a type of business that risks polluting through the use of chemicals in typical mining operations or inadequately disposing of waste material, which could include excess rocks and dirt. Typically, one would expect that a rock quarry polluted by releasing various chemicals used in the mining process, and not by releasing rocks and dirt that were used to build up a washed out road. Therefore, because a rock quarry does not typically pollute by repairing an access road with rocks and fill, the quarry in this case would not be considered a polluter with respect to this specific pollution. Although this factor would weigh toward defining various chemical discharges from the quarry as pollution, it does not similarly suggest this conclusion when the pollutants were rocks and dirt used to reinforce a road. Under the facts before the court, this factor counts against applying the pollution exclusion. In this case, considering the expectations of the parties, two factors suggest that the rocks and dirt were not pollutants and one factor weighs in favor of the rocks being pollutants. Specifically, the first factor strongly weighs against a determination of the existence of pollution because the rocks and dirt did not contain any potential chemical material. The third factor also weighs against it, but is less conclusive because a rock quarry may be commonly thought of as a polluter in numerous other circumstances. In contrast, the second factor strongly suggests that there was pollution because the rocks and dirt caused harm in the way that they were hazardous. Because two factors weigh in favor of finding the alleged pollutant to not be pollution, there would be a presumption that the rocks and dirt in this case were not pollutants covered by the pollution exclusion. Considering the expectations of the insured and insurance provider supports this presumption and suggests that the court should find that the rocks and dirt were not pollution under the exclusion. In this case, both parties would likely not expect the exclusion to apply to something that was completely natural, even though the harm caused was typical. Because of this analysis, the court would find that the rocks and dirt were not pollution as defined by the pollution exclusion.[21]

Another example of doubts about the interpretation of the insurance terms and conditions may be found in Ross. Dev. Corp v. Fireman's Fund Ins. Co.[22] In this case, the dispute concerned the classification of the material as waste. The U.S. District Court for the District of South Carolina, Charleston Division held that both the qualified and absolute pollution exclusions precluded coverage for elevated levels of metals and acidic pH conditions in the soil, groundwater, and sediment at the policyholder's former property located in Charleston, South Carolina. The U.S. Court of Appeals for the Fourth Circuit affirmed such conclusion.[23] The incident occurred on the Ashley River in Charlestone where the Planters site was producing phosphate fertiliser. The U.S. Environmental Protection Agency (USEPA) subsequently discovered environmental impacts associated with the manufacturing operations at the site, including elevated levels of metals, particularly lead and arsenic, in the soil, groundwater, and sediment, as well as acidic pH conditions. In 2005, the then owner of the property claimed the cost of remedial action incurred in accordance with regulations of Comprehensive Environmental Response, Compensation, and Liability Act (CERCLA).[24] In the course of the court proceedings, it was established that pyrite was burned on the land owned by Planters and produced pyrite slag, which was a by-product of Planters' production activities. Pyrite slag is the source of the vast majority of the arsenic and much of the lead contaminating the site. Planters disposed of the hazardous waste at the site by dumping the pyrite slag and cleaning the chambers that were used to produce sulphuric acid. Due to the arsenic contamination, there was a need to carry out remediation activities at the site. In the situation where the joint and several liability of the successive owners of the site was acknowledged, the question arose as to the insurer's liability under the insurance contract covering environmental property damage to the site. Due to the specific nature of the damage, i.e. long-term ground contamination, the insurance terms of several years (1972–1990) were taken into account.

---

[21] See Ortega Rock Quarry v. Golden Eagle Ins. Corp., 46 Cal. Rptr. 3d 517, 519-20 (Cal. Ct. App. 2006); Meeks (2009), p. 849.

[22] Ross Dev. Corp. v. Fireman's Fund Ins. Co., 910 F.Supp.2d 828 (DSC 2012).

[23] Ross Dev. Corp. et. al. v. PCS Nitrogen Inc., Case No. 12-2059 (4th Cir. 2013) (unpublished).

[24] Comprehensive Environmental Response, Compensation, and Liability Act (CERCLA) (42 USC 9601-9675).

The landlord of the site had both a contractual liability insurance agreement as owner and lesser, and a general liability insurance (CGL) agreement. The terms and conditions of insurance under which the contract was taken out included standard qualified pollution exclusions. "This insurance does not apply: (f) to bodily injury or property damage arising out of the discharge, dispersal, release or escape of smoke, vapors, soot, fumes, acids, alkalis, toxic chemicals, liquids or gases, waste materials or other irritants, contaminants or pollutants into or upon land, the atmosphere or any water course or body of water; but this exclusion does not apply if such discharge, dispersal, release or escape is sudden and accidental."

An absolute exemption was included in the terms and conditions subsequently in force (1987–1990), which read: "This insurance does not apply to: f. (1) "Bodily injury" or "property damage" arising out of the actual, alleged or threatened discharge, dispersal, release or escape of pollutants: (a) At or from premises you own, rent or occupy; (b) At or from any site or location used by or for you or others for the handling, storage, disposal, processing or treatment of waste; (c) which are at any time transported, handled, stored, treated, disposed of, or processed as waste by or for you or any person or organization for whom you may be legally responsible; or (d) At or from any site or location on which you or any contractors or subcontractors working directly or indirectly on your behalf are performing operations: (i) if the pollutants are brought on or to the site or location in connection with such operations; or (ii) if the operations are to test for, monitor, clean up, remove, contain, treat, detoxify or neutralize the pollutants. (2) Any loss, cost, or expense arising out of any governmental direction or request that you test for, monitor, clean up, remove, contain, treat, detoxify or neutralize pollutants. Pollutants means any solid, liquid, gaseous or thermal irritant or contaminant, including smoke, vapor, soot, fumes, acids, alkalis, chemicals and waste. Waste includes materials to be recycled, reconditioned or reclaimed".

The insured disputed the validity of the application of the insurer's exclusion of liability under the terms and conditions of insurance. It took the view that pyrite slag, a by-product of Planters' historic production operations at the site, was not considered waste because it had value as material for use in road construction and stabilisation. The court did not accept the arguments of the insured-polluting claimant. It took the view that the polluter's interpretation of the term "wastes" was too restrictive by focusing on whether the slag had a useful purpose not directly related to the insured's production activities. In the court's view, many by-products can be reused or recycled, giving them a certain value—in a context other than their original use. This does not mean that a by-product is not "waste" in relation to the production process in which it arose. Referring to waste as a by-product of the production process in the Ross case, the court stated that "the term "waste material" unambiguously includes pyrite slag, a byproduct of Ross's fertilizer production suitable only for low-value uses such as filling in low-lying land and road beds." Regarding the insured's argument that the absolute pollution exclusion did not apply because there was no evidence that the pyrite slag was "handled, stored, disposed of stored, disposed of, processed, or treated as waste", the district court found that the pyrite slag produced by Planter's production activities clearly fell within the definition of the term waste (Id., 835). The district court noted that the insurer's exclusion of liability specifies that waste "includes materials to be recycled, reclaimed or reconditioned", which is contrary to the position that a by-product must be completely useless or worthless to qualify as waste. In the court's view, the use of pyrite slag in a way that provided some benefit did not mean that there was no disposal. The court found that the insured's placement of pyrite slag in the ground at the site constituted "disposal" of "waste". Accordingly, any financing of "property damage" resulting from the "actual, alleged or threatened discharge, dispersal, release or escape of pollutants" on the site is excluded from the insurer's liability under the so-called absolute exclusion provided in the terms and conditions of insurance (CGL).

Similarly to Ortega Rock Quarry case, the insured also argued that pyrite slag was not a pollutant per se. He claimed that only the components of pyrite slag that were released as a result of certain environmental processes were pollutants. The insured further argued that the pyrite slag, when placed on the ground surface as fill material or road base, did not constitute a pollutant because the arsenic and lead components contained in the slag had not been released. According to the insured, "it is only when those compounds are separated from the pyrite slag that any pollutants are, in fact, discharged into the environment". The court rejected the insured's arguments, taking the opinion that the compounds contained in the pyrite slag would have entered the soil and water sources in the "normal and natural course of events without any further human action". The court also referred to the manner of release, claiming that "the fact that these pollutants may have escaped from their container slowly rather than immediately has no bearing on whether Ross discharged pollutants into the environment." In the court's view, there is no doubt that arsenic and lead do not lose their pollutant status for the reason that they are not released immediately upon discharge into the environment.

According to the insured, even if we rely on the definition used by the court, pyrite slag does not constitute "waste material" subject to exclusion from insurance protection. Pyrite slag was neither "damaged, defective or superfluous material", nor material rejected from the production process and "reclaimed" for other purposes. For the fertiliser industry, pyrite slag was a commodity for immediate use in many processes, including soil stabilisation and road construction. Their value was so high that suppliers of pyrite ore often retained ownership of the slag. From the producer's point of view, the slag was used for its "usual and main purpose", had significant value and was not waste. The insured's reasoning aimed to conclude that pyrite slag did not fall within the definition of waste covered by the so-called absolute exclusion because it was not "materials to be recycled, reconditioned or reclaimed". It argued that the slag was usable in its original state and did not need to be adapted, made ready, returned to a prior condition, restored, recovered, made available, or obtained.

The county court did not formulate a clear rule that by-products constitute waste within the meaning of the absolute pollution exclusion in the terms and conditions of the insurance in all circumstances. The court suggested that the answer depends to some extent on whether the by-product has limited value or utility, as well as whether it is a commercially valuable product. However, it emphasized that a by-product does not stop being waste by virtue of the fact that it has some value or utility. Referring to the contaminant mentioned by the terms and conditions of the insurance to include "material to be recycled, reconditioned or reclaimed", the county court emphasized that waste may have some value which does not preclude it from qualifying as waste (for the purposes of the exclusion). Logically, whether the insured's production waste pollutes the environment once it enters the environment should not depend on its degree of utility. The insured's production waste is still waste for pollution exclusion purposes, even if it has some use.[25]

The US case law on this issue, although sparse, appears internally consistent. The case of Grain Dealers Mut. Ins. Co. v. Farmers Alliance Mut. Ins. Co.,[26] concerned fly ash that had been buried by the insured on the property. The court held that the ash constituted waste as a by-product, despite the argument that it had a generally recognised productive use. Thus, the court upheld the insurer's exclusion of liability on the basis of the absolute exclusion of pollution from insurance protection.

In the case of Pipefitters Welfare Educational Fund v. Westchester Fire Ins. Co.,[27] the court examined the extent of the absolute exclusion of contamination in relation to scrap metal. The court took the view that waste that is "marketable" and still "useful" is still waste, and rejected the insured's argument that scrap metal was not waste because it was a "marketable and useful product", finding that scrap metal fell within the definition of waste, which included "material to be recycled, reconditioned or reclaimed".

In the case of Independent Petrochemical Corp. v. Aetna Cas. And Sur Co.,[28] the entrepreneur mixed the insured's dioxin waste with oils and sprayed the mixture on unpaved roads and horse arenas to suppress dust. The court rejected the insured's position that spraying of the mixture did not constitute pollution within the meaning of the exclusion in the insurance terms and conditions because the mixture was used for beneficial purposes, and argued that the waste in question was a by-product and the alleged damage resulted from its improper disposal.

The Supreme Court of California affirmed the decision of the North Carolina Court of Appeals in the case of West American Insurance Co. v. Tufco Flooring East, Inc. 409 S.E.2d 692, 699-700 (N.C. Ct. App. 1991) (Tufco Flooring), concerning the release of fumes (from styrene monomer resin) used to refinish the flooring at issue. The fumes killed livestock, so they were clearly toxic. However, the court held that the fumes were not a pollutant within the meaning of the liability insurance exclusion: "The flooring material (styrene monomer resin) brought upon the premises [by the policyholder] was wanted. It was not impure. When [the policyholder]

---

[25] La Porta (2014), pp. 348–356.

[26] Grain Dealers Mut. Ins. Co. v. Farmers Alliance Mut. Ins. Co., 2001 US Dist. LEXIS 24299, *23 (W.D.Okla 2001).

[27] Pipefitters Welfare Educational Fund v. Westchester Fire Ins. Co., 976 F.2d 1037 (7th Cir. 1992).

[28] Independent Petrochemical Corp. v. Aetna Cas. And Sur Co., 1988 U.S. Dist. LEXIS 15839 (DDC 1988).

purchased its CGL insurance, it understood "pollutant" in the same way that the Oxford English Dictionary defines "pollutant," as an unwanted impurity, not as the raw materials which [the policyholder] purchased to do its job".[29] In Tufco Flooring case, the court considered only unwanted waste to be excluded from insurance cover. The exclusion was not "meant to refer to any raw material [used] by the insured for purpose of normal business activity which accidentally resulted in property damage or bodily injury". Interestingly, in Tufco Flooring case, the court pointed to insurance leaflets, regulations and endorsements as the basis for concluding that products and completed operations were excluded from the pollution exclusion.[30] This points to the role of insurance distribution influencing the scope of the insurer's liability (see further below).

Moreover, rulings on product liability insurance also indicate that misselling is recognized and considered in cases concerning the interpretation of insurance terms and conditions. In Great Lakes case,[31] the court held that applying the pollution exclusion to injuries caused by the insured's main or primary product by characterising it as a pollutant would render much of the coverage illusory, which is an interpretation of the insurance terms and conditions that many courts have refused to enforce. The court declined to apply a literal interpretation of the pollution exclusion clauses. It declined to find that the clauses precluded coverage in this case. Great Lakes was engaged in manufacturing and selling of chemical compounds. The chemical substance in question, EDB [ethylene dibromide], was a soil fumigation pesticide designed to be applied directly to the ground. The EDB products alleged to have contaminated the soil and groundwater were applied in the exact manner intended by Great Lakes and approved by the state and federal governments. Their use and application at that time was perfectly legal. EDB was neither a by-product nor a waste product of Great Lakes. . EDB was an actual end product of the production process. Great Lakes, like most manufacturers, has taken out public liability insurance to protect itself against damage caused by its products. In this case, the damages caused by EDB were in fact environmental pollution due to the nature of the product and its intended use. Nevertheless, the fact that the alleged damages constitute environmental damages does not mean that pollution exclusion clauses should automatically apply to exclude insurance cover. The court's found that the claims made to Great Lakes were essentially product liability claims and they are not in the nature of intentional or negligent environmental pollution. The court stated that "pollution exclusion clauses bar coverage to Great Lakes for the EDB claims would render the insurance coverage purchased by Great Lakes illusory".[32]

[29] Ibidem p. 698.

[30] Ibidem at 696–697.

[31] See Great Lakes Chem. Corp. v. International Surplus Lines Ins. Co., 638 N.E. 2d 847 (Ind. Ct. App. 1994).

[32] Ibidem at 851.

It is decisions such as those above that have most likely prompted some insurers to modify their insurance terms and conditions. Many insurers have developed a product completed operations exception endorsement that they add to the pollution exclusion in the CGL policy. The intent of this endorsement is to cover products and completed operations claims involving pollution.[33] If such an exception is found in the terms and conditions of insurance that form the source of the insurance relationship, it may provide even broader coverage than in situations where the courts have recognised a product liability exception. This is because the definition of coverage for an insured product is broad and even much broader than what is considered to be the scope of traditional product liability. The "product-completed operations coverage" extends to "all 'bodily injury' and "property damages" occurring away from premises you own or rent and arising outof 'your product[.]"' What is the insured's product is broadly defined to include "[a]ny goods or products other than real property, manufactured, sold, handled, distributed, or disposed of by [the insured].". The issue here is to find the most reasonable, broad meaning of product coverage, which is a clear exception to the pollution exclusion in such insurance terms.

Whether such an exception applies to products of completed operations may depend on whether the release can still be linked to the insured's product. In Hydro Systems, Inc. v. Continental Ins. Co.,[34] the court held that the exception did not apply to waste gases or liquids generated in the manufacturing process that were no longer part of the insured's product. The court held that waste gases and liquids generated in the production process that were not part of the product, were subject to the pollution exclusion. Styrene gas was not one of Hydro's products.[35] Styrene is released during the production process of the actual completed Hydro product—fibreglass bathtubs. Hydro has never marketed styrene or made any attempt to retain it for future use or distribution. Styrene was released to the atmosphere purposefully.

US case law demonstrates that the central legal problems surrounding environmental liability insurance do not concern the theoretical insurability of waste-related risks, but rather the interpretation and application of pollution exclusion clauses in Commercial General Liability (CGL) policies. Under standard CGL terms, waste is treated contractually as a category of pollutants, and litigation therefore focuses on whether a given factual scenario falls within the scope of the pollution exclusion and how that exclusion should be applied in light of the policy wording. Cases such as Ortega Rock Quarry and Ross Development show that courts attach decisive importance to the structure and language of the insurance terms and conditions, rather than to the natural character, usefulness or economic value of the material involved. For the purposes of this chapter, this confirms that the practical limits of

---

[33] Hettrick (2009), p. 150.

[34] Hydro Systems, Inc. v. Continental Ins. Co., 929 F.2d 472, 475 (9th Cir. 1991).

[35] The meaning of the term "product" was addressed by the court in the case of CPS Chem. Co. Inc. v. Continental Ins. Co., 199 N.J. Super. 558, 489 A.2d 1265, 1270 (N.J. 1984) holding that "industrial wastes" were not products under a products hazard exception because they were "not intended for consumption, sale, or use by others . . . "

insurance protection in waste-related cases are shaped primarily by the construction and interpretation of pollution exclusions,

4.2 *Environmental Liability Insurance for Waste*

4.2.1 Pollution Legal Liability Policies (PLLs) as a Specialised Form of Liability Insurance

Pollution Legal Liability Policies (PLLs) are taken out worldwide. This name is used to describe insurance products that are an adaptation of liability insurance to environmental protection needs. Their content depends both on national or regional regulations (e.g. federal or EU) and the awareness of environmental risks and damages, including those resulting from waste management. These determinants influence the subjective scope of the clients that are offered these types of products. PLL insurance is the main type of environmental insurance available to large companies, and in some cases to small and medium-sized enterprises, provided that their availability depends on individual insurers. This broad group of entities covers waste holders as well.

The PLL policy provides coverage for costs resulting from "Pollution Conditions", which the policy typically defines as follows: "Pollution Conditions means the discharge, dispersal, release or escape of any solid, liquid, gaseous or thermal irritant or contaminants, including, but not limited to, smoke, vapors, soot, fumes, acids, alkalis, toxic chemicals, medical waste and waste materials into or upon land, or any structure on land, the atmosphere or any water course or body of water, including groundwater, provided such conditions are not naturally present in the environment in the amounts or concentrations discovered".[36] The PLL policy typically provides cover for transportation of products and waste from the insured's site (but not for products liability) and remediation of waste generated at the insured's site and disposed at an authorised waste disposal site.[37] Although the analysis begins with Pollution Legal Liability Policies as the most prominent market-based form of environmental insurance, the considerations that follow apply more broadly to liability-based environmental insurance schemes as such.

4.2.2 The Limits of Liability-Based Environmental Insurance

However, one should be mindful that this is a type of liability insurance with all the consequences resulting from this classification. The peculiarity of liability insurance boils down to the accessory nature of the insurance cover to the liability of the

[36] Zuckerman and Raskoff (2024), supra note 7, § 7:8, at 7-80 ("Pollution Legal Liability Select Policy" form).

[37] See, after Howard (2005), p. 959.

insured against third parties for damages caused to them by his or her act or omission. The property interest boils down to the protection of the insured's property in the event of his liability, the consequence of which is the compensation of the damage. So the insurers liability depends on the liability of the perpetrator (here the waste holder).

Liability insurance is predicated on the establishment of civil liability, which means that it is similarly beset by the majority of the shortcomings inherent to the civil liability rules.[38] Comprehensive insurance coverage is provided on the condition that the insured is held liable. This greatly limits the freedom to shape the scope of insurance cover.

In order to trigger causal liability, the prerequisites for liability for damages are required to be met. These are: the damage, the incident and the causal link between the damage and such incident. Liability law is a system based on causation. As a result, in every case there needs to be proof of the balance of probabilities that this specific damage was in fact caused by this act or omission. Alternative theories allowing compensation for loss of a chance or compensation commensurate with the chance of causation are increasingly applied in liability law.[39] Liability insurance, including PLL, will prove useful only where the materialisation of risk will constitute environmental damage caused by an act or omission of the waste holder. The damaged environment may not be restored or compensated in light of the difficulties associated with establishing liability.[40]

Liability systems tend not to have strict rules on damage assessment. The victim can claim "full compensation" but usually there are no lists or fixed amounts to help the insurer in this respect. As a result, calculating a lump sum award covering waste environmental damage is a very difficult task. Consequently, the cost of calculation—in terms of expertise, time and money—can prove extremely high. Thus, the apparent advantage of applying the principle of full indemnity may turn against the waste holders who bear the cost of the insurance cover (insurance premium). Contrastingly, a first party insurance would use a limited list of events in which the insurer would have to pay out and would use a list of percentages and fixed amounts. In this respect, operating a first party insurance may be less costly than a liability insurance.[41]

With regard to liability law, compensation of victims is an important goal, but not the exclusive goal. Compensation is not given to those struck by fortuitous events for which no one bears responsibility. Therefore, the objective of compensation after the event is usually connected to the aim of preventing wrongful behaviour. Underlying principle of tort law stresses that tort law also aims at providing precautionary incentives to potential tortfeasors before the event. The justification for this

[38] For a comparative analysis, see, e.g., van Dam (2006), p. 3 ff., von Bar and Drobnig (2004), p. 25 ff.

[39] Bagińska (2015), p. 43 ff.

[40] Jing (2013), p. 82.

[41] See van Boom and Faure (2007), p. 8.

principle is that if compensation of victims was the sole purpose of tort law, there would be no point in linking compensation to a specific event for which someone else bears responsibility. If the focus was in fact exclusively on compensation, then surely a more rational distribution of scarce means would have to be considered. This certainly correlates with the role that the prevention principle plays in waste management (see Chapter II). If liability law is indeed (in part) behaviour-oriented and aims at preventing and discouraging wrongful behaviour and avoidably dangerous activities by means of compensating after the event, then the general idea of this private system is that by obliging someone to compensate damage after the event, he is thus encouraged to act with the appropriate level of care before the event. Moreover, sceptics argue that there is no empirical evidence of the preventive effect of (the threat of) liability. The evidence that is available is only applicable to certain fields of the law and mainly to the legal system of the United States of America. European legal systems are to a large extent "empirical terra incognita".[42]

As indicated above, environmental damage triggers not only civil liability of compensation but also administrative obligations to restore the damaged environment.[43] The coverage adopted in such insurances may include remediation costs associated with the need to clean up contaminated land in the event of improper waste disposal as long as it is considered a damage to the victim caused by the waste holder. The question arises whether liability arising from a decision of an administrative authority (as a result of its regulatory activity) to cover such costs can be said to be the subject of this type of insurance in the case of interest. Adopting the distinction indicated in the literature between financial security for environmental liability and financial security for environmental responsibility, only the first one seem to be relevant to liability insurance.[44] It is proving difficult to use as a financial security for environmental responsibilities such as closing a landfill or restoring land following surface mining.

Information asymmetry is another formidable problem in liability insurance. To maintain the insurability of a risk, both the probability and the possible magnitude of the loss should be predictable. However, both legal and factual uncertainties exist in relation to environmental risks.[45] As a relatively new risk, environmental damage from waste may be difficult to predict due to lack of information and scientific uncertainties. There may also be uncertainty about the scope of environmental liability, given the complexity of liability rules and legal procedures.

External insurers need to address issues of moral hazard. The insurance industry has developed a whole set of mechanisms aimed at reducing the negative effects of moral hazard 17. The multitude of different instruments is based on two main strategies, i.e. monitoring the insured and/or exposing him to part of the risk. The monitoring strategy aims to eliminate moral hazard by setting the premium in exact

[42] See van Boom and Faure (2007), p. 9.

[43] Jing (2013), p. 103.

[44] Fogleman (2023), pp. 78–79.

[45] Monti (2001), pp. 59–62.

proportion to the risk borne by the insured in question. Where the insurer can determine the security measures required and observe the level of prudence actually chosen by the insured, it is able to respond to the relaxation of security measures by a proportionate increase in the insurance premium. Ex-ante rating of risks plays a major role in industrial liability insurance. In commercial liability insurance it is common for insurers to make underwriting contingent upon a thorough analysis of the risk profile of the particular installations. However, risk diversification and effective monitoring cannot be achieved without a certain price, which translates into the cost of insurance (the insurance premium). Furthermore, risk diversification necessitates the availability of extensive information, which presents a significant challenge with regard to environmental damage.[46] Under the second strategy of minimising moral hazard (exposing him to part of the risk), insurers can use deductibles or exclusions. In the case of a deductible, the incentives of the insured are partially retained as he stands to bear part of the loss herself should an accident occur.[47] Such instruments, however, limit the effectiveness of insurance treated as financial security.

A second major problem created by insurance, apart from moral hazard, is adverse selection.[48] Adverse selection denotes the fact that the demand for insurance is particularly strong among people with a high propensity to cause or suffer damage. In the context of waste insurance, the higher the probability that the incident occurs and the greater the loss incurred in case of an environmental damage, the stronger the incentive for the owner to seek out insurance protection. The fact that insurance is required as a form of financial security does not make the problem of adverse selection any easier to solve. It must be assumed that the administrative body requires financial security precisely in high-risk situations. On the other hand, requiring such security from all waste holders carrying out a certain activity (e.g. landfill managers or hazardous waste transporters) leads to risk diversification, reducing the level of adverse selection.

Like moral hazard, adverse selection thrives on informational asymmetries. If the insurance industry could differentiate accurately between high-risk insureds and low-risk insureds, then adverse selection could easily be avoided. In such a world of ideal informed insurers, the premium every individual waste holder had to pay would precisely reflect the risk run by the particular insured. In the case of little-known waste risks, pursuing this objective is particularly difficult. Technological developments affecting the redefinition of the principle of utmost good faith discussed in the broader context of the prevention principle in the second chapter should provide some assistance.

---

[46] More broadly on moral hazard and adverse selection in environmental insurance see Jing (2013), pp. 112–114.

[47] Winter (2000), p. 157.

[48] Dionne et al. (2000).

4.3 The Role of Unambiguity of Insurance Terms and Conditions

Ambiguous clauses in the insurance terms and conditions are a barrier to the development of environmental insurance and effective coverage of waste risks.[49] The client may experience negative consequences due to defects and ambiguity in the insurance terms and conditions. This is illustrated by a case involving a dispute between the insured and the insurer over the availability of funding for the insured's costs of removing construction and demolition debris that was improperly buried on the insured's property by a contractor employed by the insured to provide building demolition, site clearance and site grading services.

In Picerne case, the insured had entered into an environmental liability insurance contract with AISLIC for his property in Fort Bragg, North Carolina. Picerne has been commissioned by PBG of North Carolina, Inc. (PBG) service of demolition, site cleaning and levelling. The contractor was obliged to dispose of waste related to the performed works. The waste materials at issue consisted of "concrete, broken wood, painted wood, rebar, metal piping, white goods and vegetation (including tree trunks, tree limbs, tree stumps and mulch created from chipped trees". To achieve this goal, PBG dug large pits on the insured property, threw waste into them and covered them with soil, breaking the law. Picerne argued that all this was done without their knowledge or consent.

Sometime later, the relevant environmental authority accused Picerne of violating environmental legislation and creating a "non-conforming solid waste disposal site / open dump". The insured was obliged to stop depositing and remove all waste from this property to an appropriate disposal facility within 30 days. Costs incurred amounted to $250,000. The insurer refused to cover the costs, arguing that the waste materials in question did not constitute pollution within the meaning of the insurance terms and conditions. Pollution condition is specifically defined in the policy as "the discharge, dispersal, release or escape of any solid, liquid, gaseous or thermal irritant or contaminant, including, but not limited to, smoke, vapors, soot, fumes, acids, alkalis, toxic chemicals, medical waste and waste materials into or upon land, or any structure on land, the atmosphere or any watercourse or body of water, including groundwater, provided such conditions are not naturally present in the environment in the amounts or concentrations discovered". The court argued that the recognition of materials as waste does not in itself authorize it to be considered as contamination within the meaning of the insurance terms. It rejected the insured's arguments who referred to the common understanding of "irritant or contaminant" referring to an open list of examples that could qualify as conditions pollution. The interpretation of this concept was crucial in the case. The insurer, AISLIC, replied that there is extensive case law that defines pollution as "covering hazards traditionally considered harmful to society or the environment" and in this

---

[49] *Picerne-Military Housing, LLC v. American Intern. Specialty Lines Ins. Co.*, 650 F.Supp.2d 135 (D.R.I.09).

case the waste in question was not "hazardous and did not pose a significant risk to human health, the soil or the surrounding environment". The case was pending before the courts and did not bring a settlement favourable to the insured. The doctrine emphasizes that the solution to this problem would be a broader definition of pollution in insurance terms and conditions.[50]

Although European case law has not developed an extensive body of decisions specifically addressing the interpretation of environmental insurance policy wording comparable to that of the United States, the problem of ambiguity in insurance terms and conditions is well recognised in the jurisprudence and legislation of EU Member States. European legal systems generally impose strict requirements of clarity and transparency on insurers, particularly with respect to exclusions of liability. In Polish law, the obligation to formulate insurance terms in a clear and unambiguous manner has an explicit statutory basis. Pursuant to Article 12(4) of the Act on Insurance and Reinsurance Activity, ambiguous provisions of an insurance contract must be interpreted in favour of the policyholder. This rule has been consistently upheld by the Supreme Court, which has stressed that insurance terms may not be interpreted in a manner that deprives the insured of coverage only revealed after the occurrence of the insured event. As emphasised in Polish doctrine, excessive complexity and ambiguity of general insurance conditions may lead to the creation of merely illusory protection, undermining the protective function of liability insurance and violating the insured's reasonable expectations.[51] A similarly rigorous approach can be found in French law, where exclusion clauses must be formelles et limitées under Article L.113-1 of the Code des assurances. The Cour de cassation has consistently held that exclusion clauses which are ambiguous or insufficiently precise do not satisfy the requirement of being "formelles et limitées" under Article L.113-1 of the Code des assurances and are therefore unenforceable against the insured, with the interpretative risk borne by the insurer.[52]

At the EU level, there is as yet no uniform body of case law specifically addressing the interpretation of environmental insurance policy wording as such. Nevertheless, in Ocidental—Companhia Portuguesa de Seguros de Vida (Case C-263/22),[53] the Court of Justice of the European Union held that, in the context of consumer contracts, including group insurance contracts concluded with consumers, the contractual terms must be presented in a manner that enables the insured to become fully acquainted with them prior to the conclusion of the contract. The Court emphasised that the requirement of transparency under Directive 93/13/EEC on unfair terms in consumer contracts entails an obligation to provide the consumer with all information necessary to understand the economic consequences of

---

[50] Huenke (2013), pp. 229–232.

[51] Maśniak and Rogoziński (2021), pp. 17–30.

[52] See e.g. Cass. civ. 1re, 22 May 2001, No 99-10.889; Cass. civ. 2e, 19 February 2015, No 14-10.904; Cass. civ. 2e, 8 October 2020, No 19-11.417; Article L.113-1 Code des assurances.

[53] Judgment of the Court of Justice of the European Union of 29 September 2022, Ocidental – Companhia Portuguesa de Seguros de Vida SA v Autoridade de Supervisão de Seguros e Fundos de Pensões, Case C-263/22, ECLI:EU:C:2022:739.

contractual limitations of coverage. In particular, the consumer must have a genuine opportunity to examine the contract as a whole before being bound by it, since it is the terms of the contract taken together that determine the rights and obligations of the insured. Although the judgment concerns consumer insurance contracts and does not establish a general rule applicable to environmental insurance as such, it reflects a broader EU-level emphasis on transparency and clarity of contractual terms, indicating that ambiguous or insufficiently transparent insurance clauses—especially those defining the scope of coverage or exclusions—may be treated unfavourably where they prevent the policyholder from assessing the economic implications of the insurance protection at the time of contract conclusion 4.4. The mitigation coverage

The obligation of the insured to prevent or mitigate a pollution event are of particular importance in all insurance of environmental risks, including waste risks. Actually, attention should be drawn to the broad interpretation of the term "mitigation". The conventional meaning usually refers to actions taken by the insured to prevent pollution from becoming greater than when it was initially detected. However, "mitigation" is also required of the insured in cases "when an insured was compelled to take action to prevent a pollution event even if it has not happened".[54]

An interesting model is the Environmental Impairment Liability (EIL), also known as Site Pollution Liability coverage, widespread in the U.S. It is touted as a product that will respond to pollution conditions that become "actionable." "Actionable" generally means that something has to be done to address a pollution condition (or investigate a potential pollution condition), either as a result of new regulations, new discoveries in the area of environmental risk management or as a result of claims made against an insured".[55]

There are cases where environmental authorities amend their guidelines (e.g. landfill use arrangements or producer recycling requirements for waste equipment) by changing the standards for a certain type of activity or a certain type of waste. Discovering a new pathway for the migration of pollutants away from the disposal facility triggers an administrative decision to cease operations by the entity in question and an investigation of the property on such an entity (for example, a disposal facility) to ensure that the continuation of operations does not violate environmental regulations. In such a case, it is essential that the entity has insurance cover under the so called "discovery" (i.e. discovering a pollution condition at their location themselves) and that they notify their insurance carrier of the activities they will be conducting in order to mitigate their potential for environmental liability.

[54] Many meanings of environmental mitigation coverage (16.02.2016), https://chivaroli.com/meanings-environmental-mitigation-coverage/.

[55] Ibidem.

5 Waste First Party Insurance

5.1 Characteristics

The first-party insurance presents an option, under which insurance coverage is provided and compensation is awarded directly by the insurer to the victim.[56] Unlike liability insurance, it is the victim that takes insurance coverage to remove the risk of potential large damage to him. The compensation is awarded provided that the specific damage is a materialization of an insured risk under the insurance coverage and irrespective of whether there is liability.[57] The concept of damage boils down to the concept of loss, understood as losing, destroying or damaging the property—resulting in pecuniary loss. Insurance cover provided under first party insurance may also apply to lost profits.[58] The damage is an independent premise of the insurer's liability for damages. The waste holder can take advantage of the insurance protection for the damage they suffer themselves, for example the damage to the operator's site. Hence, the injurer and victim will be the same and it is the polluter who finances the coverage.[59] Nothing, however, precludes the insurance coverage costs from being borne by the injured party who is not the perpetrator, for example a public entity that has an interest in protecting the environment from damage caused by waste management activities.

Many scholars are in favor of first-party insurance rather than liability insurance in the sense that the transaction costs[60] are lower and risk differentiation might be easier.[61] This is related with much greater freedom of the insurer to shape the terms of insurance, in particular the subject matter and scope of insurance. Thus, it is easier to provide cover appropriate to the waste holder's needs, avoiding both under-insurance and over-insurance. In a situation where insurance coverage is required by an authority, this issue becomes particularly important.

Under liability insurance, the insured risk is that the injurer will harm a victim whose properties are unknown ex ante to the insurer. A waste environmental risk can cause damage to numerous victims simultaneously. The losses are correlated and probably catastrophic. This problem is even more serious with respect to gradual pollution. If one kind of chemical is discovered to cause latent environmental

---

[56] In liability insurance, it is only possible for the injured party to pursue compensation claims directly against the insurer if this is provided for by law (e.g. Article 822 § 4 of the Polish Civil Code). However, the insurance cover is granted to the potential perpetrator, and the injured party is not the subject of the insurance relationship.

[57] Faure and Bruggeman (2008), p. 11.

[58] See Kaliński (2021), pp. 256–266.

[59] Faure (2002), p. 295.

[60] Transaction costs are the costs of exchange taking three forms corresponding to the three stages of exchange made between the parties to the relationship. R.H. Cousy included there: (1) search costs, (2) bargaining costs, (3) enforcement costs; see Cousy (1960), p. 1; Hiofman and Spizer (1982), p. 73 f.

[61] Priest (1987), pp. 1521–1590; Bishop (1983), p. 241, Epstein (1985), p. 645.

harm, lots of claims may be made in the same period. On the contrary, first-party insurance directly covers the risk of damage with a particular victim or a particular site. On the one hand, it limits the scope of coverage. On the other hand, it is easier to identify the circumstances influencing the risk.[62] For example, with regard to the waste insurance, distinctions can be made between landfills located near or far from nature reserves or animal habitats. It is easier to tailor the insurance terms and conditions to the purpose of the insurance, such as the financial security required by the authority.

First-party insurance is financed by victims to cover their own damage. As for environmental damage, it may involve damage to biodiversity and other environmental elements, where no individual rights are directly harmed and no individuals are able or willing to assert losses (primary damage). In the case of such environmental damages per se, the injured party is the public represented by the authorities (or potentially environmental organisations) acting for the general interest. However, it is difficult to treat the environment per se as the polluting waste holder's own property. Thus, except the cases that waste holders (i.e.. industrial (mining) operators, landfill owner) seeking coverage for the possible cleanup costs on their own plant, a pure first-party insurance scheme would not be very practical for environmental damage.[63] In addition, financing of insurance cover by the victims will be exposed to criticism from the perspective of the polluter-pays principle. If the policyholder were the injured party, the problem of contradiction with the polluter-pays principle would be offset by an appropriate insurance recourse regulation. Recourse to the perpetrator of the damage outside the insurance relationship (here the waste holder) is a common solution in European legislation.[64]

To be insurable, a waste risk needs to be accidental. Accidentalness requires that damage is not the result of a deliberate choice of the insured. This would be less of a problem in the first-party insurance scheme, since most environmental accidents are of a unilateral nature. But there still exist some clues for helping to estimate the expected losses, such as the distance of specific natural resources from the potential pollution sources or the business activity an insured has.

The damage is insurable if it is caused by "an insured risk". It implies that the causation between a risk and the damage still needs to be proved. However, the difficulties in identifying a specific injurer and the uncertainties of judgments are less compared to a liability insurance contract.[65] In contrast to liability insurance based on the insurer's accessory liability to the perpetrator's liability, in first party insurance the establishment of an indemnity relationship depends on the establishment of the fact that a certain damage has occurred to a certain person, rather than on this damage happening on their property. This is because the occurrence of such damage

[62] Faure (2002), pp. 292–293.

[63] Faure (2002), p. 294.

[64] Chapter Ten: Rights of Subrogation, Article 10:101 PEICL, Principle of European Insurance Contract Law, ed. …, p. 262 et. seq.

[65] Jing (2013), pp. 124–126.

is the legal event, and must be compensated as stated in the law. Here, the debtor obliged to fulfil the contractual obligation (the insurer) is predetermined, rather than disclosed and determined by means of a causal link between the damage and the behaviour of the specific entity charged with the indemnification liability (as is the case in liability insurance). It is therefore a relationship of a normative type between a loss resulting from an insured event[66] specified in the insurance contract and a specific person obliged to compensate for this loss (insurer).[67] In first party insurance, it is also important to establish a second level of causality—the impact of the insured event on the goods and interests of the injured party, which leads to the establishment of the fact and extent of the individual damage to the property of the injured party.[68]

First-party insurance presents a specific legal and practical mechanism by which the insured may obtain coverage for damage they themselves incur, independent of third-party liability. In the context of waste management and environmental risks, this means that a waste holder—such as an operator of a landfill or an industrial facility—may secure insurance protection to cover the costs of potential environmental damage to their own site or operations. The insured event is the materialization of a risk specified in the insurance conditions, and the obligation to compensate arises upon verification of this materialization, rather than through establishing liability of a third party. This characteristic allows for tailoring insurance contracts to the particular circumstances and risk profile of the insured site, including factors such as proximity to sensitive ecosystems or the nature of the industrial activity. Importantly, this structure enables financing by entities other than the potential polluter. For example, a public authority or other entity with an interest in environmental protection may fund coverage to ensure that preventive or remedial measures are implemented, even if the authority is not itself liable for the damage. Consequently, first-party insurance provides a flexible framework that can accommodate multiple insurance interests over the same asset: the waste holder may insure their own potential costs while liability insurance or coverage for third-party benefit may address the risk of claims by other affected parties. This multiplicity of interests and coverage types demonstrates how first-party insurance can address some of the legal and practical challenges identified in the context of insurability of environmental risks, particularly those related to the measurement of loss, identification of risk, and correlation of multiple potential claims.

---

[66] According to article 1:201 PEIC, "insured event" means the materialization of the risk specified in the insurance contract.

[67] Warkałło (1972), pp. 11–112.

[68] Cf. Koch (1995), p. 4.

5.2 *Environmental Cost Insurance for Waste*

As previously mentioned, pollution caused by waste management is often unmeasurable and irreversible, and the actual value of damage to individual environmental components is generally impossible to determine and value. Therefore, the "cost" treatment of environmental damage and, consequently, of the subject matter of insurance appears to be reasonable. Meeting the requirements of insurability makes it possible to define the object of insurance as costs, including both the costs incurred to remedy the effects of pollution (cost of reinstatement) and the costs of preventive measures to prevent pollution. It may be more difficult to declare the costs of closing a landfill insurable, including the required aftercare (recital 29 of the Landfill Directive) or the costs of moving the landfill or the waste itself, unless such costs meet the condition of accidentalness.

Such insurance constitutes non-life insurance of group 16 - miscellaneous financial loss, from the point of view of the classification of insurance risks adopted on the EU market. The catalogue of insurance risks was opened by the last mentioned type of "other forms of financial loss", for which the financial loss (recorded as costs) related to waste management is eligible. Insurance of financial risks, in addition to credit insurance or business interruption insurance, can include insurance of preventive costs (to prevent pollution of environmental elements) and remedial costs (to restore the environment to its pre-pollution state—rehabilitation or land reclamation) associated with waste management.

Treating expenses as a financial damage that creates an obligation to pay compensation is confirmed by the forms of damage distinguished in the common law system. In addition to general damages, specific types of damages are distinguished, which include loss of profit and expenses. Expenses refer to the costs that the injured party had to incur as a result of breach of contract or tort. Expenses are aimed at restoring the state before the breach. The costs incurred by the injured party constitute a drawdown of their assets by actually diminishing their items of value. Expenses incurred by the injured party knowingly and intentionally constitute an element of the damage suffered by them.[69] The possible allegation that the damage represents a drawdown of assets that occurred against the will of the injured party can be countered by the declaration that, although the expenses were incurred knowingly by the injured party, the injured party was forced to incur them. expenses were not incurred voluntarily by him.[70] The "cost" treatment of damage is also related to the permissibility of compensating so-called pure economic loss, which are not linked to personal injury or damage to property.[71]

The direct damage caused by the deterioration of natural resources often comes down to the costs of conservation and the costs of restoring the environment to its pre-pollution state. Compensation for preventive measures should include the

[69] See Warkałło (1972), pp. 129–130.

[70] Cf. Szpunar (1999), pp. 31–32, Z. Radwański (1997), p. 83.

[71] Silverstein (1999), p. 403 ff, Parisi et al. (2006), p. 2 ff.

reimbursement of all necessary and appropriate expenses incurred to preserve natural resources, prevent damage or reduce its extent. Assessing which measures should be considered necessary and expedient depends on the type of environmental elements at risk of pollution and the type of harmful waste management activity. The entity most competent to carry out such an assessment is the authority that carries out the public tasks of environmental protection (more on the role of the authority is discussed in the last section of this chapter).

The realisation of the compensatory function of first party insurance used in waste management for the environment protection should come down primarily to the costs incurred to restore the elements of the environment to a state as close as possible to their pre-pollution state. However, clean-up costs should not only be understood as the costs of minimising the impact and severity of the damage immediately after the accident, but also the long-term costs of restoring natural resources. The costs of reinstatement should be understood as any measures taken to restore or reinstate damaged or destroyed elements of the environment, or to introduce the equivalent of such elements into the environment (where this is reasonable). The scope of coverage of such costs should not be limited to the costs actually undertaken, but should also include costs that need to be undertaken in the future.

Such an insurance contract implies an obligation of the insurer to finance specified (for example, in an administrative decision) costs both where preventive and/or remedial measures have been carried out by the insured (or on their instructions), and where such measures have been ordered by an authority (e.g. the competent environmental authority). Due to the difficulty of determining the injured party in the case of environmental damage, the focus should be put on the subject matter, i.e. the activities included in the form of costs. The insurance instrument based on the guarantee (and not causal) liability of the insurer focuses on the damage suffered. If we consider the specific costs resulting from the waste holder's damaging activity as such a damage, it is no longer relevant who ordered the financing of the activity (restoration or rehabilitation) covered.

The "cost" treatment of the subject of insurance makes it easier to address the problem of compensation for changes in environmental elements that are the result of gradually increasing contamination. This type of damage involves the difficulty of proving the staggered processes that are the source of the damage. The difficulty in proving the premise of environmental damage and its extent results from the continuity of their occurrence and revealing themselves after a long period of environmental impact. It concerns essentially primary environmental damage. Rarely does this type of damage arise as a result of a single event.[72] Public entities (state treasury, local government units) that represent the public interest have the entitlement to bring claims for such damages. Defining an insured event as the issuance during the insurance period of a final decision of a competent authority (authority) to allocate funds from the financial security to cover the costs of substitute performance resolves this problem. Insurance cover is provided for the costs of substitute

[72] Cf. Maśniak (2003), p. 233.

performance for the restoration of the condition from before the pollution that are causally related to the insured event defined above.

Perceiving the subject of insurance as costs generally reduces the problem of determining the sum insured to the will of the parties based on an assessment of the risk and the policyholder's ability to pay. When treating an insurance contract as required by the financial security authority, the first factor mentioned will arguably prove crucial. Although it cannot be excluded either that the waste holder—policyholder will have an influence on the amount of financial security to be imposed. As mentioned earlier (chapter three), the EU legislator takes a cautious approach to imposing the amount of financial security required. Some guidance in this type of insurance may be the agreed value insurance.

The insured value is determined on the basis of a so-called *"valuation"* which is an appraisal made by experts appointed for this purpose by the insurance company and/or the policyholder at the contractual stage. This method is often used when establishing the actual value is troublesome for evidentiary reasons. The doctrine draws attention to the possibility of establishing an agreed value for an object that has no monetary value at all.[73] This approach makes it possible to construct an insurance contract in which the environmental elements are the subject matter. Despite the fact that the value of the insured environmental elements has not been agreed, the insured value can be agreed as the basis for determining the sum insured, which should correspond to the amount of financial security required.

6 Distribution of Waste Insurance

As of October 1, 2018, European Union member states had to enact the necessary legislation to implement Directive 2016/97 of the European Parliament and of the Council (EU) of January 20, 2016 on insurance distribution (IDD. The IDD was born out of a desire to provide customers with equal protection regardless of the type of distributor from which they obtained insurance. In essence, the IDD aims to level the playing field for insurance customers by simplifying, consolidating and extending customer protection where necessary. The IDD aims to focus on the "area of disclosure" to customers to enable them "to make an informed decision" (Article 20 IDD). The IDD seeks to achieve the goal of enhancing customer protection by ensuring greater transparency of insurance distribution with regard to the price and costs of insurance products, requiring better and more comprehensible product information, and improving conduct of business rules, with particular attention to advising. The doctrine has attempted to compare the solutions adopted in the IDD with the model laws promulgated by the National Association of Insurance Commissioners (NAIC) in the United States.[74] The IDD is unquestionably focused

[73] Cf. Warkałło (1969), p. 73.

[74] Martinez and Marano (2020).

on customer protection. The NAIC is more concerned with uniformity. Unlike the NAIC Model Acts, the IDD are comprehensive with respect to customer protection.

The preamble of the IDD directive (recital 44) indicates that the obligation for insurance distributors to carry out a demands-and-needs test is an expression of the pro-consumer trend in European insurance law.[75] This is evidenced by the wording of the preamble to the IDD which indicates that, in order to avoid cases of mis-selling, the sale of insurance products should always be accompanied by a "demands-and-needs test on the basis of information obtained from the customer. Any insurance product proposed to the customer should always be consistent with the customer's demands and needs and be presented in a comprehensible form to allow that customer to make an informed decision" (motive 44). Therefore, Article 20 of the IDD should be considered crucial for pre-contractual customer protection. Article 20 provides that any contract proposed shall be consistent with the customer's insurance demands and needs. Thus, prior to the conclusion of an insurance contract, the insurance distributor shall specify, on the basis of information obtained from the customer, the demands and the needs of the customer. Where advice is provided prior to the conclusion of any specific contract, the insurance distributors shall provide the customer with a personalized recommendation explaining why a particular product would best meet the customer's demands and needs.

The EU legislator makes it clear that both demands-and-needs test and advice, including "a personalised recommendation explaining why a particular product would best meet the customer's demands and needs" shall be modulated according to the complexity of the insurance product being proposed and the type of customer. The demands and needs analysis boils down to identifying the risks involved. If the person seeking protection is a waste holder starting their business, the relevant risks associated with their activity will be the risk of environmental responsibility and liability. The obligation to obtain financial security mobilises the waste holder to take care of the protection to the extent imposed by law and specified by the administrative authority. The requirement for financial security is a customer requirement, the disclosure of which is the purpose of the distributor's demands and needs analysis. Thus, the risk of environmental liability is clarified by the obligation to provide financial security as a condition for the waste holder to start or continue operations.

In the case of environmental insurance, and in particular insurance related to waste management, the customer's demands and needs are not shaped exclusively by the customer's own assessment of risk, but to a significant extent by legal and administrative requirements imposed by public authorities acting on behalf of local government units and the State Treasury, as beneficiaries of the insurance arrangement in a broad sense. These authorities condition the commencement or continuation of waste management activities on the provision of adequate financial security. As a result, the demands-and-needs analysis performed by the insurance distributor must take into account not only the interests of the waste holder as the contracting party, but also the regulatory expectations of the competent authority assessing the

[75] See Ziemiak and Marszelewski (2017), pp. 100–116.

sufficiency and acceptability of the insurance cover. This specificity directly affects distribution processes, requiring insurance distributors to align the proposed insurance product with administrative acceptance criteria, rather than solely with the individual risk preferences of the customer.

The demands and needs analysis, crucial to making an informed decision on insurance protection, should lead to coverage for environmental risks in the broadest sense, including liability for both primary damage and secondary damage affecting the interests of private parties. An important risk for the waste holder is also the risk of loss of income that may be caused, for example, by a decision to close a landfill and the risk of legal costs. Waste management is carried out with the help of machinery, whose undisturbed operation also affects the risk of responsibility.

Fulfilling its obligation (Article 20 of the IDD), the insurance distributor informs the customer about an insurance product adequate to their requirements and needs. In the case discussed, this adequacy should be understood in two ways: (1) the insurance contract provides financial security, the conditions of which will be deemed sufficient by the licensing authority to permit the management of waste activities, (2) the insurance cover protects the assets of the waste holder against drawdown in the event of environmental damage and the resulting consequences qualified as both environmental responsibility and environmental liability.

Analysing the demands and needs of the waste holder will certainly show some needs, other than the environmental ones. As a result, such a client may be offered a single comprehensive insurance product covering several risks, including those required for financial security. Distribution can also amount to offering a couple of insurance products, one of them being specifically designed to meet the conditions of financial security. In both cases, the provided coverage goes beyond the specific risks required by the legislator/authority, focusing on the protection of public funds in situations that threaten the environment (i.e. closing a landfill or restoring land following surface mining).

The activity of insurance distributors boils down to qualifying the customer into a particular target group for which the insurer (as the insurance distributor) has developed the terms of protection. Thus, the distributor's activity boils down to the assessment of risk associated with the waste holder's business. As a developer of insurance products—where standardised general terms and conditions of insurance are the most essential element—the insurer or intermediary (e.g. an insurance broker) focuses on the risks associated with a specific type of waste management. Waste management encompasses various types of operations (chapter one), which differ significantly from each other from the point of view of the environmental risks that translate into the demands and needs of waste holders.

Hence, the insurance market offers recycling insurance which and provides comprehensive protection for the waste holder running a recycling operation, covering environmental costs, liability insurance, business interruption, property insurance (machinery, equipment or infrastructure of the recycling plant). For marketing and distribution reasons, distributors bundle insurance products covering different types of insurance related to the operations of a given entity. Hence the difficulty in interpreting the term used by the EU legislator in the WEEE Directive. It identifies "recycling insurance" as one form of guarantee required from producers to secure the financing of costs for the management of WEEE from orphan products. In this sense, recycling insurance should be understood as an insurance covering both the costs of recycling: collection and transport of waste equipment, treatment and recycling of materials, disposal of non-recyclable components and liability for damage caused by inappropriate waste management.

7 The Environmental Authority as an Entity Outside of the Insurance Relationship

For the sake of conceptual clarity, it should be emphasised that references in this chapter to the "authority" do not concern the authority as an autonomous legal subject. The authority acts solely as an administrative body exercising public powers on behalf of a public-law entity, namely the State Treasury or a local government unit. It is these public entities, endowed with legal personality, that bear the economic and legal consequences of environmental damage and whose interests are protected by the requirement to provide financial security. The authority's role is therefore limited to the exercise of regulatory, supervisory and enforcement competences within the framework of administrative law, whereas the protected interest underlying the financial security belongs to the public entity represented by that authority.

The financial security required of the waste holder at the stage of undertaking its activities is intended to provide the necessary funds for environmental remediation, even in the event of the waste holder's bankruptcy. In this way, the financial security reduces the risk that the state will have to bear the cost of remediation, allocating public funds for this purpose. The adequacy of this financial security, which takes the form of an insurance guarantee and/or insurance contract, is examined by the same body that is in the process of issuing environmental permits and is in the possession of the regulatory authority (most often the local government administration).[76]

In such a case, the role of the administrative body can be seen in three stages. In the first stage of verification of the security, the authority issuing the administrative decision to carry out specific management activity assesses whether the terms and conditions of the insurance meet the requirements set out in the legislation. The second stage is monitoring of the security continuity. The authority verifies that the security is valid for the entire period of waste management. Finally, the third stage, which may or may not occur, is the use of the security. In the event that an entity fails to meet its obligation to dispose of the waste or repair the damage, the authority may use the financial security in the form of insurance. The wording of the

[76] For example in Germany, a specific act (Kreislaufwirtschaftsgesetz) requires waste holders to establish financial security to cover the costs associated with the installation closure and any remedial action – Kreislaufwirtschaftsgesetz (KrWG) § 36 KrWG and 48 for hazardous waste. An assessment of the adequacy of this security is carried out by the competent authority issuing the waste permit.

insurance terms and conditions may also indicate that the use of the financial security, i.e. the payment of compensation in this case, may also occur if the authority decides to outsource the execution of certain activities (waste removal, land reclamation) to an entity other than the waste holder—policyholder without waiting for him to fulfil his obligations. Guided by the principle of prevention, and taking into account the specific nature of environmental damage, this use of the financial security should be considered justified.

Verification of insurance as adequate financial security takes place prior to or coinciding with the conclusion of the insurance contract. As previously mentioned, the purpose of insurance as financial security should already be considered at the pre-contractual stage, as part of the demands and needs analysis. Nothing prevents the terms and conditions of the insurance to be consulted by the waste holder—policyholder with the competent authority. This helps avoid a situation in which the authority finds that such a security does not meet the requirements, and demands other security (e.g. a bank guarantee or a deposit—see the second chapter) from the waste holder. The admissibility and legal validity of such consultation with an authority will depend on the public law (administrative law) national regulations.

It is worse for the next stage of the authority's participation in the implementation of financial security—monitoring the financial security continuity. In the case of an insurance contract concluded by the waste management licence applicant, the waste holder authority remains outside of the insurance relationship. It could only have certain entitlements if the contract is concluded for someone else's account and the authority is named as the insured. In the latter situation, his interest is covered and, according to European legislation, the insured should be informed of the conditions that affect him and can directly claim compensation from the insurer.[77] However, he never becomes a party to the insurance contract and has no influence in this respect on the policyholder, who may decide to terminate the insurance contract. A certain limitation in this respect is treating the insurance contract as a fixed term contract, which in principle should not be terminated before the expiry of the insurance period. This period should be correlated with the duration of the waste management licence. Furthermore, the terms and conditions of insurance contract may limit the freedom of the parties in this respect. One possible way to address this problem is to exclude, within the insurance contract, the right of termination, to the extent permitted by non-mandatory law, or to stipulate in the insurance contract an obligation to notify a third party (the administrative authority) of events affecting the continuation of insurance cover, particularly where the right of termination is statutory and of a mandatory (ius cogens) nature. Another possible solution is to grant the administrative authority a power of attorney enabling it to obtain access to information covered by insurance secrecy, insofar as such access is necessary to verify the existence and continuity of the financial security Unfortunately, neither of these solutions excludes termination by mutual agreement of the parties, which

[77] According to Article 11: 101 PEICL (1), in the case of an insurance taken out for a person other than the policyholder, if the insured event occurs, that person shall be entitled to the insurance money.

cannot be excluded. Unlike in the case of insurance as a mean of securing loan repayment, here the public entity represented by the authority is not bound by a contract that could be terminated in the event of termination of the insurance contract. In this case, we also have the difficulty of linking a private-law relationship with a public-law relationship.

The third stage of the authority's participation, i.e. the use of insurance cover as a security, is related to the difficulty that may arise in relating the administrative-legal decision that entails the obligation to cover preventive and remediation measure costs to the content of the insurance terms and conditions and their interpretation by the insurer. As previously mentioned, the authority is not the subject of the insurance relationship, which creates a risk for both parties: the authority and the insurer. On the one hand, the authority has no influence on the use of the security, which is determined by the insurance terms and conditions, but also by no less important interpretation of these conditions by the insurer. On the other hand, the insurer may fear that the content of the administrative decision on the obligation to cover preventive and remediation measure costs will not be adequate for the insurance risk assumed by the insurer. The insurer is not a participant in the administrative proceedings before the authority. The policyholder, on the other hand, does not necessarily care about limiting the amount of costs imposed by the decision. This is an example of moral hazard, where the validity of the insurance contract may influence the behaviour of the waste holder as a participant in the administrative proceedings.

References

Bagińska E (2015) Kompensacja utraconej szansy – problem związku przyczynowego czy szkody? In: Olejniczak A, Haberko J, Pyrzyńska A, Sokołowska D (eds) Współczesne problemy prawa zobowiązań. Wolters Kluwer, Warszawa

Bailey Kathy D, Gulledge W (1997) Using environmental insurance to reduce environmental liability. Nat Resour Environ 11(4):26–30

Basedow J, Birds M, Clarke H, Cousy H, Heiss H, Loacker L (eds) (2016) Principles of European insurance contract law (PICL). Sellier European Law Publishers GmbH, Köln

Bishop W (1983) The contract-tort boundary and the economics of insurance. J Legal Stud 12:241

Byczko Sz (2013) Interes ubezpieczeniowy. Aspekty prawne, Difin 71–75

Cousy RH (1960) The problem of social cost. J Law Econ 3:1

Dionne G, Doherty N, Fombaron N (2000) Adverse selection in insurance markets. Montreal

Epstein RA (1985) Products liability as and insurance market. J Leg Stud 14:645

Faure M (2002) Environmental damage insurance in theory and practice. In: Swanson T (ed) An introduction to the law and economics of environmental policy: issues in institutional design. Elsevier Science, Oxford

Faure M, Bruggeman V (2008) Catastrophic risks and first-party insurance. Connecticut Insur Law J 15:11

Faure M, Liu J (2018) Risk-sharing agreements to cover environmental damage: theory and practice, risk-sharing agreements to cover environmental damage: theory and practice. Int Environ Agreements-Polit Law Econ 18(2):259

Fogleman V (2023) Environmental liabilities and insurance law in the European Union. In: Maśniak D, Malinowska K (eds) Managing environmental risk through insurance. Springer
Hettrick CM (2009) Everything is relative, including the "Absoluteness" of the current. Restrictive Pollution Exclusion. Environ Claims J 21(2):150
Hiofman E, Spizer M (1982) The coase theorem: some experimental tests. J Law Econ 25:73f
Howard WH (2005) New issues in environmental risk insurance. Tort Trial Insur Pract Law J 40(3):959
Huenke AD (2013) Environmental insurance policies are negotiated contracts and not commodities. Environ Claims J 25(3):229–232
Jing L (2013) Compensation ecological damage. Comparative and economic observation, Cambridge
Kaliński M (2021) Szkoda na mieniu i jej naprawienie. C.H. Beck
Kisch W (1933) Ubezpieczenia. Książka i Wiedza, Warszawa
Koch A (1995) Związek przyczynowy w ubezpieczeniach, PA, 3:4
Kowalewski E (1997) Wprowadzenie do teorii interesu ubezpieczeniowego. In: Wąsiewicz A (ed) Ubezpieczenia w gospodarce rynkowej. Torun-Bydgoszcz
La Porta AJ (2014) A waste is a waste is a waste: if it polluted it should be excluded. Environ Claims J 26(4):348–356
Martinez L, Marano P (2020) The new EU rules on insurance customer/policyholder protection viewed against the NAIC model acts. Global Jurist
Maśniak D (2003) Ubezpieczenia ekologiczne. Kraków
Maśniak D, Rogoziński D (2021) Limits of insurers' freedom in shaping coverage in liability insurance for entrepreneurs. Prawo Asekuracyjne 1(106):17–30
Meeks Ch (2009) The pollution delusion: a proposal for a uniform interpretation of pollution in general liability absolute pollution exclusions. George Wash Law Rev 77:828
Monti A (2001) Environmental risk: a comparative law and economics approach to liability and insurance. Eur Rev Priv Law 59–62
Parisi F, Palmer VV, Bussani M (2006) The comparative law and economics of pure economic loss. George Mason University School of Law Working Paper Series Year Paper
Priest G (1987) The current insurance crisis and modern tort law. Yale Law J 96:1521–1590
Radwański Z (1997) Zobowiązania – Część ogólna. Warszawa
Rejda G (2017) Principles of risk management and insurance, Global Edition. Pearson Education Limited
Silverstein E (1999) On recovery in tort for pure economic loss on recovery in tort for pure economic. Univ Mich J Law Reform Univ Mich J Law Reform 32:403
Smith M, Witt R (1985) An economic analysis of retroactive liability insurance. J Risk Insur 52(3) September 1985
Szpunar A (1999) Odszkodowanie za szkodę majątkową. Szkoda na mieniu i osobie, Oficyna Wydawnicza Branta
van Boom WH, Faure MG (2007) Introducing "shifts in compensation between private and public systems". In: van Boom WH, Faure MG (eds) Shifts in compensation between private and public systems. Springer, Germany
van Dam C (2006) European tort law. Oxford University Press
von Bar C, Drobnig U (2004) The interaction of contract law and tort and property law in Europe – a comparative study. European Law Publisher
Wagner G (2007) (Un)insurability and the choice between market insurance and public compensation systems. In: van Boom WH, Faure MG (eds) Shifts in compensation between private and public systems. Springer, Germany
Warkałło W (1969) Ubezpieczenia majątkowe. PWE
Warkałło W (1972) *Odpowiedzialność* odszkodowawcza. Funkcje, rodzaje, granice. Warszawa
Wettersteinn P (1997) Proprietary or possessory interest: A 'Conditio Sine Qua Non' for claiming damages for environmental impairment. In: Wetterstein P (ed) Harm to the environment: the right to compensation and the assessment of damages

Winter R (2000) Optimal insurance under moral hazard. In: Dionne G (ed) Handbook of insurance. p 157
Żebrowska A (1997) Ubezpieczenia ekologiczne a ochrona środowiska naturalnego. Wiadomości Ubezpieczeniowe 3–4:3
Ziemiak MP, Marszelewski M (2017) Selected remarks on policyholders protection in the draft of Polish act on insurance distribution. Rozprawy Ubezpieczeniowe 3:100–116
Zuckerman TI, Raskoff MC (2024) Environmental insurance litigation: practice forms. Clark Boardman Callaghan

Conclusion

The analysis leads to the conclusion that from a legal point of view insurance is an instrument for rational and ecological waste management. Insurance should be used in an efficient and well-organized approach to waste management. Insurance activities can support the efficient use of resources and minimisation of waste generation that is required as part of a sound planning and management strategy. Appropriately applied insurance-legal institutions support environmental protection, being part of waste management practices that prevent harm to human health and damage to the environment. This general conclusion needs to be complemented by more specific questions pointing out the legal and insurance barriers to the development of waste insurance in its broadest sense, and how to overcome them.

Waste risks are a very diverse group associated with a wide range of activities classified as waste management. Its distinction is hampered by the relative status of waste and the difficulty in distinguishing waste from product (including by-product). The case law of the Court of Justice helps, but does not resolve all doubts. In the search for waste management instruments, it is important to think in terms of the waste hierarchy shaped by EU law, and to treat waste as a type of residue. As evidenced by EU and US legislation, the greater the environmental risks associated with waste management, the greater the intervention of the legislator. From the point of view of environmental impact, the type of waste is not insignificant, hence the particular interest of the legislator in hazardous waste.

When thinking about waste risks, it's important not to lose sight of the notion of production and environmental protection. The difficulty associated with waste management results from the strong link between this activity and production. Hence the need to manage risks in a way that reasonably achieves the environmental objective while taking into account the economic objective. Insurance is considered the most effective way to manage risks, as long as the risks can be qualified as insurance risks. Not all waste management risks can be recognized as pure risks, which, unlike speculative risks, we consider to be insurable. Waste management generates

D. Maśniak, *The Legal Framework for the Use of Insurance in Ecological Waste Management*, AIDA Europe Research Series on Insurance Law and Regulation 17, https://doi.org/10.1007/978-3-032-26550-0_7

speculative risks, i.e. risks of a dual nature that takes into account the possibility of gain—profit from the activity. Hence, the type of waste management associated with waste hierarchy is of such importance for the qualification of waste risks as insurance risks. Not all types of waste management equally generate insurable waste risk. Landfilling classified the lowest in the waste disposal hierarchy will be most affected. It does not mean that recycling does not involve insurable waste risks, but to a greater extent they go beyond waste as an environmental risk.

Waste as environmental risk represents pure risk, which can take the form of liability risk, personal risk or property risk.[1] The waste holder's point of view, waste as environmental risk takes the form of liability risk for environmental damage. Liability risk applies to the waste holder in a broad sense. From the point of view of the injured party, waste environmental risk takes the form of both personal and property risk. The personal risk associated with the personal rights infringement (such as health or ability to work) concerns victims who are natural persons. They are also threatened by property risks. The focus, however, is on compensating for so-called primary environmental damage directly affecting the environment. W ich przypadku poszkodowany reprezentowany jest przez authority, a ryzyko sprowadza się do ryzyka pokrycia odpowiednich wydatków. In their case, the injured party is represented by the authority and the risk is reduced to the risk of covering the relevant expenses. When there is imminent threat of waste environmental damage if damage occurs, further damage should be prevented by appropriate measures, and it is not sufficient to simply to clean up and restore the area. Restoration is a method of transforming damage to un-owned natural resource into a monetary loss suffered by the person who took the restorative measures. Restoration helps to individualize the collective interests that have been infringed and thus the damage can be classified as a pecuniary damage. An example of restoration of environmental damage is soil remediation due to a damage caused by waste management, if the remediation is carried out by a specialised entity on the basis of a administrative authority's decision. The cost of such restoration could be covered by the polluting waste holder's insurer.

The paradigm shift in insurance law and insurance practice from risk transfer to risk prevention is an important factor in strengthening the role of insurance in waste environmental risk management. The law prevention principle—key to environmental law—is becoming increasingly important in the insurance business. Prevention of insurance in waste management is linked to their social impact and the possibility of supporting state action in this area. Thinking in terms of prevention should merge into all stages of insurance coverage (insurance distribution, insurance contract conclusion, contract execution). The importance of the prevention principle is reinforced by its connection to the classic principles of insurance law—the principle of good faith and the principle of indemnity—as well as the other principles identified in the monograph as reinforcing the use of insurance in waste management.

---

[1]According to E.J. Vaughan's classification, E.J. Vaughan, T. Vaughan, (1999), Fundamentals of risks and insurance, John Wiley and Sons, p. 7.

The impetus for seeking insurance cover is provided by two principles focusing on entities responsible for the environmentally harmful effects of waste management. The first is the Waste Holder Pay Principle which is a modification of the Polluter Pay Principle. An interpretation of EU law has led to the conclusion that, despite differences in legal terminology, the term "waste holder" captures the personal scope of a potential waste managing polluter most accurately. By "waste holder" we also mean a manufacturer whose responsibility covers the entire life cycle of a product. The Extended Producer Responsibility Principle ensures that the producers bear financial and/or organizational responsibility for the management of waste. Thinking of a product in terms of waste, the management of which is a phase in the entire lifecycle of the product, is a great and costly challenge for a producer. The transfer of risk to the insurer seems to be a way of dealing with such a challenge. The need for financial security in the event of insolvency of an electrical and electronic equipment manufacturer has already been recognised by the EU legislator. The circular economy model based on the "repair, re-use, recycle" scheme extends the life of a product. Identifying it more strongly with the product, it changes the way we think about waste. This model reduces the generation of waste and promotes types of waste management that can be considered environmentally friendly, with the consequent reduction of waste environmental risks. It correlates closely with The Extended Producer Responsibility Principle by focusing on risks associated with the entire life cycle of a product. This monograph focuses on the use of insurance as an instrument for protection against waste environmental risks. The implementation of the Extended Producer Responsibility Principle and the Circular Model Economy reveals insurance needs related to widely understood waste risks associated with liability of manufacturers and other waste holders who provide services that extend the life cycle of a product (such as business interruption or product liability).

There is an apparent tendency in both Europe and the United States for legislators to interfere in waste management by imposing financial security. It supports rational and ecological waste management. In expanding the objective and subjective scope of compulsory financial security, legislators indicate types of waste or waste management that give rise to particular waste environmental risks. Linking financial security and treating it as a condition for activities that create waste environmental risk is a positive phenomenon.

An analysis of EU law leads to the conclusion that a shortcoming of the point-based approach is the lack of consistency in clarifying and defining the admissible forms of financial security, which makes it difficult to implement and develop the standards needed in this area. Without questioning the differences between types of wastes and waste management, the regulations glaringly lack correlation with the conceptual apparatus of insurance law. Ultimately, there is a burden on the Member States to adapt their national laws in such a way that financial security is an efficient instrument for the authority unfamiliar with legal and financial instruments. A rational financial security instrument is one that takes both environmental and economic considerations into account.

The requirements of specified waste holders to have insurance protection—or another type of financial security—raises awareness of environmental liabilities. The requirements for permit waste holders to provide financial security are in place to protect society, i.e. taxpayers, from the risk of having to bear waste management costs, including restoration costs. If a permit waste holder enters bankruptcy or is for some other reason unable to fulfil their obligations, the financial security they have provided must be sufficient and able to be used for financing the measures required to carry out those commitments. The amount of the financial security constitutes an operating cost for the operator. The amount needs to be balanced so that it discourages landfilling as the least environmentally sound form of waste management, but at the same time does not encourage illegal landfilling or transport due to overly strict requirements.

The various forms of financial security indicated in the legislation are all classified as personal security. Insurance actions are not a universal remedy for all situations in which the legislator has recognised the need for financial security, even for one type of waste management. It would not be justified to restrict the choice of admissible forms to insurance activities only. However, it is important that the choice of financial security type does not come down to the simplest and least complicated solution (such as security deposit), which is at the same time the most financially severe for the waste holder. Insurance activities are adapted to economic reality while fulfilling a guarantee function. It is also important who should choose the form of financial security. Given the purpose of financial security, it is difficult to question the role of the authority who represents the public interest that is the subject of the security. However, one should be mindful that such security represents a real financial burden for the waste holder—the cost of the undertaken economic activity. The public-law relationship between the authority and the waste holder does not exclude allowing the waste holder to choose the form of financial security, provided that the chosen form fulfils the conditions set by the legislator or by the authority.

The insurance business is a response to the needs of waste environmental risks management if it is recognised that it does not simply boil down to a regulated insurance contract, often incorrectly identified with insurance. The specificity of waste risks determined by social considerations specified in environmental law is the impetus for the development of waste guarantee insurance. With many similarities to an insurance contract, it is characterised by greater freedom in shaping the content of the legal relationship. Guarantee insurance can be an alternative to an insurance contract both because of its lower cost and less rigorous requirements for the insurer's performance. The obligations of a tripartite guarantee insurance relationship can be more closely aligned with the financial security requirements of administrative decisions. Insurance contract may be used to provide cover for the risk of landfill or waste facility closure whose costs exceed the estimated costs, the operator being required to close the landfill or waste facility before the planned date for doing so, or environmental damage from incidents during closure or aftercare. A guarantee could be used to cover the estimated costs of closure and aftercare. This is because the insurance protection under the insurance contract covers fortuities, but not certainties. According to principle of indemnity, indemnity is a guarantee to restore the insured to the position he or she was in before the uncertain incident that caused a loss for the insured.

Like the insurance contract, the insurance guarantee is based on a community of risk, which is an organisational feature of the insurance business. The community of risk specific to insurance relationships allows for remuneration based on an insurance premium that corresponds to a diversified risk. Even if a "commission" (not a "premium") is charged for issuing the guarantee, it is calculated taking into account the risk of the guaranteed event.. For such a non-standard activity as waste management, building such a community is not an easy task. The obligatory scope of financial security and a distribution that takes into account both types of insurance products corresponding to both insurance activities are helpful in this respect. Including a specific waste holder in the target customer group makes it possible to inform the waste holder about the alternative in the form of an insurance contract and an insurance guarantee, or to recognise that only one of the mentioned types of insurance products will be adequate for the waste holder's needs as a customer. In practice, often the individual situation of the customer determines the choice between the two insurance actions. This matter is the advantage of an insurance guarantee over a bank guarantee, which is structurally very similar.

An insurance guarantee is a relationship based on three legal relationships. As a way of securing environmental waste risks, waste insurance guarantee covers three legal relationships: 1. the so-called basic legal relationship between the waste holder (obligor) and the authority—beneficiary of the guarantee, 2. the relationship resulting from the contract linking the waste holder (obligor) and the insurer (guarantee application), and 3. the guarantee relationship (guarantee contract between the authority (beneficiary) and the guarantor—insurer. The unregulated nature of the insurance guarantee makes it possible to assume that the relationship referred to in point 1 does not have to be of a civil law nature, but may be of an administrative law nature. Furthermore, the relationship referred to in point 3 may be based on a unilateral act in law, and not on a contract.

Looking at its function, a guarantee is related to a suretyship. The primary function of a guarantee is to secure claims for damages based on reneging, to secure the performance of a monetary claim arising from a legal relation. However, in contrast to a suretyship, a guarantee is legally independent from the underlying legal relationship. A guarantee is therefore generally seen as a stronger form of security than a surety which is accessory in nature, as it establishes independent liability for the principal obligation. A guarantee does not reinforce the underlying relationship as does a surety, but serves to compensate the beneficiary for a loss, since the guarantor is not liable for the debtor's debt as in the case of a surety, but for obtaining a guaranteed result. In the case of waste insurance, guarantees should be granted at the request of the waste holder when applying for a waste management permit to secure claims (claims for the cost of performance related to the removal of waste from a site not intended for storage and/or the repair of environmental damage). Such performance guarantees are intended to protect the environmental authority or another authority from failure to implement an administrative decision to bear the cost of certain remedial actions.

The existence of insurer's recourse claim against the debtor (waste holder) is the most important difference between an insurance contract and an insurance guarantee, affecting the level of the insurance risk assumed by the insurer, which translates into the insurance premium. The possibility to assert a recourse claim against the waste holder allows the guarantee commission/premium to be shaped at a lower level than the premium in the insurance contract.

The compensatory nature of insurance contract results in the lack of possibility to cover risks whose materialisation do not result in a damage. An example of such a risk is the closure of a landfill site and/or relocation to another site. However the guarantor's liability is not compensatory in nature, as its purpose is to achieve a given result and not to redress a damage. The beneficiary does not have to prove the damage while exercising a claim under the guarantee. The indicated difference between the two insurance instruments shows the advantage of an insurance guarantee as a possible financial security in such a case. It should be noted that the failure to achieve the expected result secured by the guarantee contract constitutes a loss for the beneficiary, compensated by the payment of the guarantee sum. Although its payment does not constitute a typical compensation, it fulfils a compensatory function.

The analysis leads to the conclusion that, despite their long history and considerable popularity, liability insurance is not a rational instrument in waste management. It applies to commercial liability insurance which generally does not cover damage caused by waste. Additional difficulties are caused by terminological uncertainties and ambiguous clauses in terms and conditions forcing judicial enforcement of claims, as exemplified by the extensive US case law. However, there is also criticism of environmental liability insurance, which, although shaped with environmental risks in mind, remains a type of liability insurance with all the limitations of this type of insurance. Liability systems tend not to have strict rules on damage assessment. It is inadequate for the scope of liability imposed by the authority on waste holders obliged to provide financial security.

The preferred insurance solutions for the protection of environmental waste risks are insurance guarantees and Environmental Cost Insurance for Waste (ECIW), constituting first party insurance. A guarantee provides security in the event of the loss of financial liquidity of the waste holder—debtor. A financial insurance contract (ECIW being a type of which), can play the same role. The key difference between the two boils down to the bilateral or tripartite nature of the established relationships. This influences the level of involvement of the third party which—in the area under study—is the authority. Its role stems from the fact that insurance is treated as a form of financial security, which of course is not the only option for the use of insurance in waste management. In the case of ECIW imposed by an authority representing the public interest, the issue is the inability of an environmental authority outside the insurance legal relationship to influence the content of the insurance terms and conditions shaping the scope of insurance coverage. The use of an insurance for a third party's benefit is one of the solutions to support the use of

ECIW. It allows the potentially polluting waste holder to be charged for the insurance premium while naming the authority as the insured.

Reference

Vaughan E.J., Vaughan T (1999) Fundamentals of risks and insurance. John Wiley and Sons.

MIX
Papier aus verantwortungsvollen Quellen
Paper from responsible sources
FSC® C105338

If you have any concerns about our products,
you can contact us on
ProductSafety@springernature.com

In case Publisher is established outside the EU,
the EU authorized representative is:
Springer Nature Customer Service Center GmbH
Europaplatz 3, 69115 Heidelberg, Germany

Printed by Libri Plureos GmbH
in Hamburg, Germany